CHINA FASHION

CHINA FASHION

Conversations with Designers

Christine Tsui

Oxford • New York

English edition
First published in 2009 by
Berg
Editorial offices:
First Floor, Angel Court, 81 St Clements Street, Oxford OX4 1AW, UK
175 Fifth Avenue, New York, NY 10010, USA

Berg is the imprint of Oxford International Publishers Ltd.

Library of Congress Cataloging-in-Publication Data

A catalogue record for this book is available from the Library of Congress.

British Library Cataloguing-in-Publication Data

A catalogue record for this book is available from the British Library.

ISBN 978 1 84520 514 0 (Cloth)
978 1 84520 515 7 (Paper)

Typeset by Apex CoVantage, LLC, Madison, WI, USA.
Printed in Great Britain by the MPG Books Group, Bodmin and King's Lynn

www.bergpublishers.com

CONTENTS

ILLUSTRATIONS

ACKNOWLEDGEMENTS

This book was compiled using primary research through interviews with prominent fashion designers in China. To ensure its quality and accuracy, most of the designers were interviewed more than three times, a few five or six times. The majority of the interviewed designers are the most influential design professionals in China. As such, they are often engaged in various social events and activities, in addition to their heavy workloads with their own brands or companies, so I thank them greatly for taking time out of their busy schedules for the book.

Due to the Cultural Revolution in the 1960s through the 1970s, scarce resources were available in the historical archives. Thus, for their contributions of invaluable historical information and documentation, I am grateful to Jin Tai-Jun, who has worked in the industry since the 1940s, as well as the post-Mao first-generation designers, most of whom were born in the 1950s.

I interviewed ten designers for this book. Listed in the order their interviews appear, they are Jin Tai-Jun, Wang Xin-Yuan, Wu Hai-Yan, Liu Yang, Frankie Xie, Liang Zi, Ma Ke, Wang Yi-Yang, Lu Kun and Ji Ji.

Special thanks are due to Zhang Zhe and his wife Fang Ming, and also Ye Hong and Zhang Zu-Fang. All of them have worked in the clothing industry since the 1980s and are respected experts in the industry. They helped me connect with some of the interviewees, and provided me with resources for my research.

Thanks are also due to the photographers. Without their beautiful visual recording of the designers' artworks, it would be hard to imagine what the fashion world would look like.

Kevin Manley and his wife Melissa deserve my most special personal regard. I have worked for Kevin for six years, and we developed a great friendship through our work. His wife Melissa, a writer who has published several novels, recommended the professional editor Sherrie Holmes to me.

My publisher, Berg, produces academic books and journals focusing primarily on visual culture, including the world of fashion. I made initial contact with Berg through a short e-mail query—a quick note asking if the company would be interested in a book about the history and development of Chinese fashion designers. They responded the next day, having foreseen the rising trend in Chinese fashion, and asked me to send a proposal. I did, and from there it went through several steps, including reader assessment and submission to management for approval, submission of sample chapters . . . and now, here is the final product. Great thanks to Hannah Shakespeare, who was my first contact at Berg, and Anna Wright, who replaced Hannah when she left the company. Appreciation is also due to Julia Hall, who is the in-house editor for this book. I guess it takes more effort to edit a book written by a foreigner! Emily Medcalf is responsible for the cover design. Publishing a book is about teamwork, and I'm sure there are many other heroes and heroines behind the scenes whose efforts contributed to the publication of this book. I salute these unknown people, too!

The book would not have qualified for publication without the editorial assistance of Sherrie Holmes, a freelance editor in the United States. To take the writing of a non-native English speaker and transform it into proper English takes special expertise. In addition to correcting the linguistic and grammatical mistakes, Sherrie helped me clarify passages that may have been unclear to Western readers—something that would have been difficult for me to notice as a native of China.

All contributors to this book are greatly appreciated!

PREFACE

As one of the most economically promising countries in the world today, China is attracting more attention from the international communities in all aspects. But very little is known about Chinese fashion, although the country is the largest clothing manufacturing centre in the world. China has undergone dramatic changes in the past three decades, but few people outside of China know the history of Chinese fashion and how that history has affected the development of native fashion designers. Chinese fashion designers have dreamed of establishing designer labels in Western markets since the first generation of designers became prominent. Yet, despite this prominence in the inner fashion circles of China, the designers had trouble breaking into the mainstream Western market.

China is unique, given her political system and economic infrastructure, her 5,000 years of history and culture, her enormous population, the aggressive growth of her GDP—gross domestic product—and the fact she is the largest clothing manufacturer in the world. How will these special characteristics influence the growth and design personality of Chinese fashion designers? How will their experience and personalities differ from designers who grew up in a Western culture? Will Chinese fashion designers have the potential to establish labels worldwide and became a promising force in the international market? Will we see the 'ones' from any of the three generations in the near future? With the current trend toward globalization, what role shall or will the Chinese fashion designers play in the world?

I hope this book will help answer some of these questions.

1 INTRODUCTION

Fashion, as the reflection of culture, history and the socio-economic status of a nation, has always been an important and fascinating subject. The world's interest in fashion can be attributed, at least partially, to fashion designers, a group of people who dare to challenge the old rules and create a new vision for clothes.

Recognized as the largest garment manufacturing centre internationally, China is generally regarded as a country that can only make or copy clothes, rather than actually create fashion. Even within China, the public media and mainstream markets are dominated by Western names and international brands. Many believe that China has few fashion designers, including numerous Chinese people who have enough financial power to consume major brands such as Louis Vuitton, Gucci and Chanel, but who, paradoxically, are not familiar with the names of local designers, regardless of the fact that these designers have gained fame in the inner circle of the fashion industry in China.

It is difficult to track down any in-depth information about Chinese fashion designers from publicized information. Most of the information available about designers gives only basic facts such as date of birth, schools attended and awards. If a few designers are fortunate enough to be interviewed, they are asked only routine questions such as, "Where did you get your inspiration from?" or very broad questions such as, "When are we going to see Chinese fashion brands outside of China?"

Chinese clothing designers are a force that cannot be neglected in the realm of fashion today. As a group of creative people who live in a country with the fastest economic growth on the planet, Chinese fashion designers are more eager than ever to demonstrate their capability to the world, becoming more active in international fashion shows in cities like Paris, Seoul and Hong Kong. Furthermore, younger designers, having successfully created their own brands, have moved into mainstream shops in cities such as Beijing or Shanghai, which have, historically, carried only foreign brands. An example is the line Exception, created by designer Ma Ke, which has become one of the most influential designer brands in the local market since its inception more than ten years ago.

However, times are changing, and, due to its rapid economic growth, China is attracting enormous attention today. The world is opening up to Chinese designers, and many are venturing out of the country with their designs; some young designers are preparing to introduce their designs in department stores such as Galeries Lafayette in Paris and Selfridges in London.

Given that China is a state with a unique political and economic infrastructure, a nation that has 5,000 years of history, a country that has the largest population in the world, it is accurate to state that Chinese fashion designers have grown up in a complex, unique environment. Thus, they are creating clothing designs that clearly feature Chinese characteristics, which, in theory, will differentiate them from those born in the Western world.

Hence, this book presents a broad picture of the development of Chinese fashion designers, incorporating the history of China from the pre-liberation period of 1911–1949 to the thirty-year anti-fashion period beginning in 1949 and the later economic reform period that started in 1978. This book will also analyse the characteristics of Chinese fashion designers, how these qualities were formed, how they have affected the development of the designers, and how they will affect future trends in the fashion market in China and the rest of the world.

This book comprises interviews with ten selected top fashion designers in China, chosen for their reputation and achievements. Each designer tells a story about his or her personal experience that will cover his or her personal life, education, career development and the process of creating his or her designer brand in China. In addition to these interviews, the book details areas that have influenced the development of Chinese fashion designers, including the Chinese fashion education system, fashion events (fashion week, fashion design contests), fashion media, the retail market and fashion enterprises.

The designers included are not only the most influential and well-known in China, but they have also had valuable experience in brand building within the Chinese market. This distinction is critical in terms of understanding the development of Chinese fashion designers, because it is difficult to evaluate a designer's work if the designer has not had a connection to, and the support of, an established brand.

The interviewed designers were selected, in part, for their diversity in terms of geographical region (north, central and south), gender and age, with the focus on those born from the 1950s through the 1980s. In addition, this book will differentiate between those with a formal fashion education, either local or overseas, and those who never received any professional training.

Designs with different signature styles will be covered, including both masculine and feminine designs, body-hugging gowns, architecture-influenced clothes, designs modified from traditional Chinese costumes and those inspired by Western or Japanese designers.

The selected designers represent the essence of the history of Chinese fashion designers. As such, the book will not only help fashion researchers in fields of history, culture and design to understand the evolution of Chinese fashion designers, but it will also be invaluable for fashion entrepreneurs and fashion managers who are interested in expanding into the Chinese fashion market by enabling them to learn about Chinese fashion culture's consumption traditions and working philosophy.

A BRIEF HISTORY OF CHINESE FASHION DESIGNERS

Following Chinese history, the development of Chinese fashion designers can be divided into three major phases: pre-liberation (before 1949), the fashion forbidden period (Chairman Mao era) and the post-Mao era (since the 1980s).

PRE-LIBERATION
Tailors: The Birth of the Western Tailoring School

Prior to the liberation of the Chinese people in 1949, *tailor* was a more popular word than *fashion designer*. This is very similar to the history of Western fashion designers. In Paris, the oldest fashion capital, most designers started as tailors or couturiers, and in the early days, there was very little difference between a tailor and a designer with regard to the work they performed.

Like many other places in the world, prior to the 1940s, most Chinese had their clothes made rather than purchasing them from retail stores. In old China, there were two major schools of tailors. One was *Ben Bang*, meaning 'Chinese tailoring school', which comprised a group of tailors who made traditional Chinese robes or jackets.

Conversely, when the government of the Qing dynasty opened coastal cities, making them more accessible to Western countries, many merchants from overseas immigrated to cities like Shanghai, Tianjin and Guangzhou. Some of these Western merchants engaged in the tailoring business, and these foreign tailors hired local Chinese people to be their apprentices or workers and taught them the techniques of Western cutting. Also, some of the Chinese tailors learned cutting skills by repairing Western-style suits for foreigners. This group of tailors later became *Hong Bang*. In Chinese, *Hong* means *red*. The popular explanation about the use of the word *red* is that, in the eyes of old Chinese people, Westerners had white skin and red hair, so in a broad sense *red* referred to *foreigners*.

The major difference between traditional Chinese tailoring skills and Western tailoring skills is that traditional Chinese tailoring schools did not have much knowledge of pattern cutting. As examples, the words *dart* and *cutting line* were tailoring terms later brought to China by Western tailors when they immigrated to old China. In addition, the old Chinese tailors were not familiar with the concept of 'modelling', a method of using a dummy to do cutting. This explains why at this time all Chinese costumes looked flat in shape. According to the tradition, Chinese tailors cut directly on one piece of fabric, with one hole at the top for the head and the other two holes on the side for the armholes. Despite their lack of cutting skills, old Chinese tailoring schools specialized in fine craftsmanship. An examination of historical pictures of Chinese costumes shows that all costumes were embellished with delicate embroideries or intricate decoration on the collars, hems and cuffs.

Hence, immigration of Western merchants to China brought new knowledge to Chinese tailors, greatly influencing their tailoring methods. As an example, *Qi Pao*, a Mandarin gown worn by Chinese women, illustrates how Western cutting skills have impacted Chinese tailoring.

Qi Pao originated from *Manchu*[1] in the Qing Dynasty. At the very beginning, *Qi Pao* was used as riding wear. This dress was made with one piece of fabric in a simple flat form with no darts or cutting lines. When old Chinese tailors learned pattern-cutting skills from Western tailors, they realized that darts would help reduce the volume difference between the hip girth and waist girth and that fabric could be cut into different pieces, and then assembled to form different shapes. So, they added darts and cutting lines to *Qi Pao*, leading to its modern manifestation, which, unlike the old *Qi Pao*, shows the body shape of women and makes the appearance of the garment more feminine.

Fashion: Popularity of the Western-style Suit

Also influencing the evolution of Chinese costumes was the fact that more Chinese young people went overseas to study or work, and more immigrants from overseas moved to China. The East–West culture collision gradually changed the lifestyle of the Chinese people. More young people, especially those who were educated in Western countries, switched their daily wear to Western-style suits.

The outbreak of the Revolution of 1911 destroyed the Qing regime and established the Republic of China. The transition to political sovereignty spread Western fashion to a broader area of China. As people tried to distance themselves through their clothing from the social and political associations of the Qing Dynasty, Western-style suits automatically became more popular in this period.

Not long after, the new trend of wearing Western-style suits raised objections from the traditional Chinese textile millers. The popularity of the Western suits, normally made from wool, seriously affected the sales of traditional Chinese fabrics such as silk and cotton. A long public debate regarding the style of dress the Republic of China should adopt to mark the birth of a new era while avoiding a negative impact

Figure 1.1 Wax figure: *Ben Bang* tailor. Image courtesy of Ningbo Museum of Costume (Ningbo is the place where the *Hong Bang* tailors originated).

Figure 1.2 *Ben Bang* tailor shops in old China. Image courtesy of Shanghai Archive Centre.

Figure 1.3 There were many Western merchants in the early
twentieth century in Shanghai. Image courtesy of Shanghai
Archive Centre.

on the national textile industry ensued. Finally, in October 1912 (Wang 2003: 92),
the government of the Republic of China officially announced the 'Formal Dress
Code of the Republic of China'. The new regulation defined men's formal wear as
a Swallow-tailed Coat and/or *Cheong Sam,* and suggested that women wear knee-
length tunic-like tops with a pleated skirt. The style was a mix of the traditional
Mandarin gown and Western fashion.

 After the Revolution of 1911, fashion went to two different extremes. At one
end, people worshipped the Western-style suits because they symbolized a new era
and a new statement of dignity, though at the same time putting traditional Chinese
silk and cotton millers at risk of bankruptcy. At the other end, the legacy power of
the Qing Dynasty tried to retain the old empire and costume. Thus, people's attire
became partly a political symbol. Because of this, creating a new dress code for the
Chinese people became part of the political agenda for Sun Yat-Sen, the first provi-
sional president of the Republic of China. Sun Yat-Sen, inspired by Western suits and
Japanese military uniforms, created a new type of suit called the *Zhong-Shan suit.*

 The *Zhong-Shan suit* adopted the cutting form of Western-style suits, with the
features of a turn-down collar, four symmetrically placed flap pockets, five buttons on

Figure 1.4 *Qi Pao* in the early twentieth century. *Qi Pao* in the early days had no darts and cutting lines in the waist and bust. Image courtesy of Ningbo Museum of Costume.

Figure 1.5 Exquisite Chinese embroidery. Image courtesy of
Ningbo Museum of Costume.

Figure 1.6 Wax figure: A Chinese woman is working on embroidery. Image courtesy of Ningbo Museum of Costume.

the central front and three buttons on the cuff. The overall style symbolized the political ideology of the new sovereignty: the symmetrically placed pockets represented the core of Chinese culture—balance and harmony; the five buttons symbolized the five divisions of the government—administration, legislation, judicial, examination and control; the three buttons reflected the core principles of the new authority, which was strongly influenced by the philosophy of Abraham Lincoln: that is, to be the government 'of the people, by the people and for the people'.

In general, the openness of China to Western countries and the constant revolutionary changes within affected the overall lifestyle of the Chinese people. These social conditions stimulated the rapid growth of *Hong Bang* tailors, and more traditional Chinese tailors switched to making Western-style suits and/or *Zhong-Shan suits*.

Formation of a Fashion Centre and the Earliest Chinese Fashion Designers: Shanghai
Birth of Women's Fashion Tailors

Because of its easy access, open culture and concentration of Western embassies and merchants, and as one of the coastal cities that first opened to the Western world,

Shanghai became the fashion centre of old China. Most tailors who made Western-style suits in old Shanghai were able to communicate directly with foreigners in English, while nowadays it is difficult to find such a tailor or even designer in China. Language skills helped these old tailors learn the advanced technology and management skills from Western businessmen, while Hollywood movies, English fashion magazines, Western ballroom dancing and other elements of the Western lifestyle strongly influenced the daily wear of Chinese young people.

The proliferation of Western fashion stimulated the growth of *Hong Bang* tailors, and eventually generated the earliest Chinese fashion firms. To *Ben Bang,* the traditional Chinese tailoring school, there wasn't much difference in how clothes were made for men and women. But when many traditional *Ben Bang* tailors switched to *Hong Bang,* they found that creating a form for women differed greatly from a men's form. A new branch named *Hong Bang* Dressmakers was formed and split from *Hong Bang* tailors. *Hong Bang* Dressmakers focused on women's wear with a range of suits, dress and gowns, whereas *Hong Bang* tailors only produced the typical Western men's suits.

Based on documents preserved by the Shanghai Archive Centre, the first person who learned cutting skills for Western women's jackets in China was Zhao Chun-Lan. Indeed, he is regarded as the father of fashion in China. Born into a tailor's family in the 1820s in Shanghai, Zhao, as a child, was sent to serve a church. Later, in 1848, he travelled to the United States with a pastor and learned cutting skills for women's clothes there. After returning to China, he taught Western cutting skills to his Chinese students.

When the fashion business grew larger, *Hong Bang* Dressmakers started to extend their business from made-to-measure to ready-to-wear and opened chain shops at different locations. At the same time, they changed the name from *Tailor's Shop* to *Fashion Shop.* Hong Xiang, regarded as one of the most influential fashion firms in old China, is a good illustration of the history of the first group of fashion firms in China.

Hong Xiang: The First Fashion Firm in China

Hong Xiang, founded in 1917 by two brothers in Shanghai—Jin Hong-Xiang and Jin Yi-Xiang—was the first company to term itself a 'fashion' firm in China. According to Jin Tai-Jun, the son of one of the founders, the word *fashion* (in Chinese *shizhuang*) was first created by an old literati friend of the founders that meant 'the clothes fit the times'.

The two brothers, who both came from *Hong Bang* backgrounds, were the fourth-generation students of the aforementioned father of fashion, Zhao Chun-Lan. Like many other tailors, the two brothers were born into a poor family and started as apprentices when they were teenagers. They received no formal education. Neverthe-less, the two brothers were smart, open-minded and sociable. During their appren-ticeship, they not only mastered all the tailoring techniques, but they were also able to remember all the likes and dislikes of the clients along with their contact informa-tion. They spent all their spare time learning English. When they had enough money to start their own business, they built the first fashion firm in the country in 1917 and named the company after the elder brother—Hong Xiang Women's Fashion Firm.

Looking back now on Hong Xiang's development, it is surprising to see how closely this top-ranked Chinese fashion company followed the same business model as many international brands. Hong Xiang was the first firm to use the founder's name in the name of the company, very much like what Chanel or Dior did with their own brands in Paris. All other Chinese tailors in the same period either used a Chinese pronunciation of an English name because of their fascination with Western culture, or used traditional Chinese words like *Chang*, which means 'prosperity' or *Xiang*, which means 'harmony'. Hong Xiang was also the first to adopt an advanced Western organization structure, and created positions for designer, fitting model and

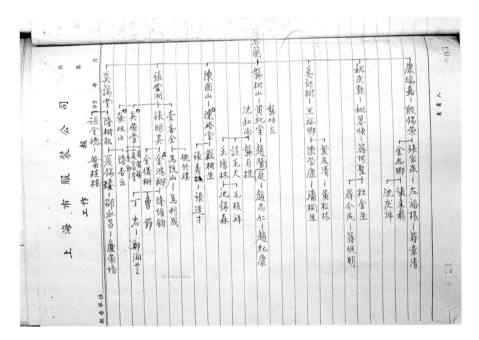

Figure 1.7 The pedigree of the father of Chinese fashion Zhao Chun-Lan and his students. Image courtesy of Shanghai Archive Centre.

window dresser. According to Jin Tai-Jun, heir of the company, the three positions were filled by Jews from Jewish refugee camps in Shanghai.

In addition, the two brothers were excellent at taking advantage of celebrity endorsement and sales promotions. They used film festivals or celebrities' birthdays to send free dresses as gifts to movie stars, or they promoted their own name through fashion shows. For instance, at the request of the central government, Hong Xiang made a typical red Chinese wedding costume in 1947 for the wedding of Queen Elizabeth—then Princess Elizabeth. The costume included a top jacket and a pleated skirt, embroidered with a giant filigree phoenix, a typical Chinese totem that symbolizes 'queen'. The costume was packed in a black lacquer wood box and sent by the younger brother, Jin Yi-Xiang, and his son, Jin Tai-Jun, to Princess Elizabeth through the British counsellor in Shanghai. Not long after, Hong Xiang received a thank-you letter with a personal note from the princess. Hong Xiang made a copy of the wedding costume and displayed it at its shop, together with the letter from the princess, and received enormous attention from the local media. Unfortunately, treasured historical records like this were all destroyed later during the Cultural Revolution. Hong Xiang was also the first marketer in the fashion history of China who encouraged customers to buy, issuing buy-one/get-one-free coupons.

Because of its trendy designs, excellent craftsmanship and advanced management concepts, Hong Xiang attracted socialites, movie stars and wives of government officers and wealthy men. It soon became a well-known fashion brand in Shanghai. People saw the name of Hong Xiang in books and newspapers and saw movie actresses in Hong Xiang clothes. The label was regarded as a luxury brand, because the high prices meant that only wealthy people could afford to buy fashionable clothes.

Hong Xiang's influence on Chinese fashion was profound. The famous First-class Fashion Firms in Shanghai were formed by the eight top fashion companies, including Hong Xiang. All the other seven owners had worked for Hong Xiang prior to the establishment of their own businesses. The honour of First-class was awarded to the eight fashion companies because of their high level of service, superior quality of products and the fame they achieved in the market. All of their shops were located on the high-end fashion street, Nanjing Road, the equivalent of Bond Street in London and Champs-Elysées Avenue in Paris. Based on the regulations in place at the time, only First-class Fashion Firms were permitted to open shops on Nanjing Road. The eight First-class Fashion Firms formed a club and met regularly to discuss the trends influencing the next season. Hence, these firms automatically played the role of fashion leaders throughout the country.

In 1928, the elder brother, Jin Hong-Xiang, formed the first fashion council in Shanghai with support from his friends and the government. The council aimed to execute policies from governmental departments such as the Industrial and Commercial Department and the Tax Bureau, conduct market research, gather feedback from

Figure 1.8 The Hong Xiang Shop on Nanjing Road in old Shanghai (Nanjing Road in Shanghai is the equivalent of Bond Street in London). Image courtesy of Shanghai Archive Centre

the members and coordinate issues between unit members or employers and labourers (Archive Q243–4-1, the Shanghai Archive Centre). The council was disbanded after the liberation in 1949.

Suffice it to say, Hong Xiang was one of the most influential fashion companies in the history of China. However, its successful business model was discontinued after liberation, and the only one who continued the fashion business in Jin's family and became the company's sole legacy was the son of the founder, Jin Tai-Jun. One of the first generation of teachers to educate young Chinese fashion designers, Jin Tai-Jun was a great contributor to the Chinese garment industry.

Jin Tai-Jun: The First Fashion Designer in China

Jin Tai-Jun, born in 1930, was asked to join his father's company when he was thirteen years old, right after his graduation from one of the most famous junior middle-schools in Shanghai. In the first several years at the company he served as an apprentice and learned cutting skills from his father and other senior tailors in the company. Later, he learned fashion drawing and design principles from the Jewish fashion designer.

When asked about how he designed at that time, Jin said it was very similar to how Western designers worked. To ensure the designs kept pace with international trends, the company subscribed to fashion magazines like *Vogue* and *Harper's Bazaar* and purchased pattern blocks from overseas. Hollywood films were another inspirational source. Jin often went to theatres to see what was in vogue internationally based on the costumes the actresses wore in the films. He usually went to the theatre early in order to give himself time to learn what was in mode on the streets by observing what theatre-goers were wearing.

Normally, Jin first illustrated the clothes that were in his mind and then cut the pattern with a combination of modelling cutting and flat cutting skills. 'After the pattern was cut, I always spent time checking it on a dummy to make sure the proportion was right and the shape was properly cut,' said Jin. 'You need to check it from a distance, otherwise you miss the overall shape of the garment. It is important to keep in mind that fashion design is a combination of creativity, art, cutting skills and craftsmanship. It is hard to believe a designer with no knowledge of cutting can be

Figure 1.9 The Certificate of Appointment appointing Jin Tai-Jun to be the fashion designer. Issued by the Shanghai government in September 1979.

a good designer.' As a designer who grew up with a tailoring background and, later, as the educator who trained many younger designers for new China, Jin was strongly opposed to designers who regarded fashion drawing as the whole of fashion design and had no desire to learn the technical component of making clothes.

The Interruption of the Fashion Era

In Jin's generation, besides the eight First-class Fashion Firms, other famous fashion shops included *Bong Street* (in Chinese *Peng Jie*), a firm founded by a Jewish business-man and later changed to a Chinese state-owned company, and *Yun Shang*, which was built by three female socialites.

In general, growth of local fashion firms and the influence of foreign fashion merchants made fashion a prosperous venture in China at this time. However, fashion was facing a tortured road ahead when the future of the oldest and largest oriental country veered towards a new, restrictive era.

1950–1970: THE FASHION FORBIDDEN PERIOD
Uniforms Era

After the Liberation War (1945–1949), the new China conducted a series of movements and campaigns to restore the economic and industrial infrastructure that had been severely affected by the war. At the same time, they worked to eradicate the legacy power of the bourgeoisies, specifically those who owned private businesses before the liberation, and to build a completely new socialist country. In 1956 the Planned Economic System[2] was formed; under this system, all private companies, including fashion shops like Hong Xiang, were purchased by or merged with state-owned companies. China entered into an economic era that was entirely controlled by the state government.

The shortage of materials led the government to introduce the Coupon System in 1954. Under this system, coupons were issued based on the number of people in each family, and these were used to purchase basic items for living, including fabrics, food and home furniture. The system lasted thirty years, up until 1984.

The constant political reform and new movements, together with the physical and economic constraints, greatly changed the cultural ideology of Chinese people. Clothes were a political statement, so in the first few years of the 1950s, the Mao-suit and the Lenin-suit uniforms became the most popular attire of Chinese people.

Since Chairman Mao was on the board of the new Chinese government, one of the *Hong Bang* tailors, Tian Jia-Dong, was assigned to make a suit for him. Tian made

Figure 1.10 Mao-suit made by Tian Jia-Dong (replica). Image courtesy of Ningbo Museum of Costume.

some alterations based on the *Zhong-shan suit* so the garment would be suitable for Mao's physically large size and his image as the leader of a large country. The tailor widened the collar, altered the corner of the collar from round to square and enlarged the overall size of the suit. Per Chairman Mao's request, Tian added a hole on the top right pocket for a pen to express the virtue of education to the Chinese people.

The Lenin-suit, worn by Lenin, became popular in China because the former Soviet Union was regarded as the prototype of the new China, since it was then the first and largest socialist country. The Lenin-suit was very similar to the *Zhong-shan suit* except for its double breast and waist belt; it was worn by many Chinese men and women until the break-up between the former Soviet Union and China at the end of the 1950s.

By the end of the 1950s the negative effects of the war and political movements gradually subsided. From the newspapers and documents preserved by the archive centre, it is evident that by the mid-1950s people's daily wear showed signs of changing. With the nation's economy in recovery, and with help from the national and municipal governmental departments, Shanghai organized a Garment Fair of Women's Wear and Children's Wear. The aim was to provide a more colourful variety of clothing to women and children, since in the previous few years they had all worn the same uniforms as men and it was not 'fit for the image of China as a great socialist country' (Wang 2003: 175). Based on a report written 29 February 1956 in one of the oldest and most popular newspapers in China, *Xinmin Wanbao* ('*New People Evening Paper*'), the fair featured more than 600 design illustrations contributed by fine arts workers, clothes designers and senior garment technical workers (Zhu 1956: 2). Two-hundred-fifty of the designs were chosen for women's clothes and fifty for children's wear. The women's designs covered clothing for daily wear, holiday wear, evening wear, sports wear, maternity wear and working uniforms. Perhaps to promote the image of the working-class (who were regarded as leaders and pioneers of the Proletariat), working uniforms were the key category at the fair and successfully presented styles for women who worked in many different industries, including hospitals, schools and the food industry.

In pictures from the early 1960s it can be seen that, by then, people had better choices in what to wear. The Western-style suits were back in style; women wore more colourful and feminine dresses and hairstyles were more flexible. However, just when people started to see a glimpse of light, the nightmare of the ten-year-long Cultural Revolution began. Suddenly, what to eat, wear, say and do were all attached to a revolutionary spirit and following the state prescriptions was regarded as patriotic. During the Cultural Revolution, hair, jackets and trousers that were too long would be cut to a 'proper length'. Even the width of the trouser cuffs needed to be carefully cut to a proper size. Western suits, blouses and dresses became a symbol of the bourgeoisies, regarded as a serious political statement of the wrong kind. Military uniforms in colours of army green, dark blue or grey, together with an emblem of Chairman Mao, became the only proper thing to wear. No country has ever been influenced so dramatically, across such a large geographical area and long period of time, over people's daily wear as has China by this revolution.

The Cultural Revolution not only changed people's view on clothing, but worse, it created a break between China's traditional cultures, which sprang from 5,000 years of history, and its later development. During the Cultural Revolution, knowledge was considered a sin and the annual entrance exams to universities were cancelled. Schools, research centres and factories were closed so people could contribute time to the revolution. Fourteen million urban youths were sent to the countryside to live and work with peasants as a result of the Rustication Movement[3]. Numerous books, photos, documents and artefacts were burned or destroyed. The Cultural Revolution eventually resulted in a high illiteracy rate and the severe collapse of the national economic power. For that same reason, this book contains very few pictures dated earlier than 1980.

Destiny of Fashion Firms and Designers

After liberation, all the older fashion firms either went bankrupt or changed from the fashion business to making uniforms. In the 1950s, many clothing firms were transformed into factories and started to manufacture clothes and export them to socialist countries, most significantly, the former Soviet Union. But after a break with that nation in 1959, China started exporting to capitalist countries. With its advantages of excellent workmanship and a huge population of workers and cheaper labour costs, China was in the initial phase of forming its image as a world manufacturing centre.

It is widely thought that from the 1950s to the early 1980s there were no clothing designers in China. In fact, clothing design was still an active profession prior to the 1980s. For instance, costume designers still did clothing design for most of the popular theatrical drama groups or films during this period. Clothing designers could still be found in garment research centres. For instance, the aforementioned designer Jin was moved to the No. 15 Garment Factory to be in charge of the exporting business to the Soviet Union, since Hong Xiang was acquired by the state. A few years later he was charged with responsibility for the Shanghai Garment Research Centre, the only clothing unit in Shanghai authorized to receive visitors from overseas and take orders from them at the time. During this time, Jin also designed window display clothing to demonstrate Chinese design capabilities to visitors from overseas. He also designed clothing for the national exhibition.

Prior to the 1980s designing clothing was just an ordinary occupation, like any other job. Clothing designers were looked upon as a group of people similar to tailors. It was after the late 1980s that clothing designers gradually gained attention from the public and clothing design became fascinating work to individual designers.

Here are examples of the life of clothing designers in China prior to the 1980s.

Based on information found in the Shanghai Archive Centre, since the economic system was totally state-controlled, people's motivation and enthusiasm for work faded because regardless of an individual's contribution, everyone was paid the same meagre wage. Egalitarianism was the general philosophy. After all, different rates of pay would create the rich and the poor, which went against the philosophy of a great socialist country. In addition, a pervasive political ideology dominated the overall management philosophy. As such, a worker who gave his or her full support to the building of a great socialist country was given greater encouragement than those workers who had high skills but no political sense.

The following citation was adopted and edited from a business report written in 1956 by the Shanghai Apparel Group. This group acquired most of the fashion firms built pre-liberation in Shanghai, making it one of the largest state-owned garment enterprises in China, both then and now. The report was meant to summarize the business performance of past years and, obviously from the tone of the report, it can be concluded that the overall performance was quite disappointing.

> In history, design was a critical factor in the growth of the apparel industry; it determines the success or failure of an enterprise. Before the liberation, fashion companies focused on sourcing new fabrics and creating new styles for customers. Design involves both art and science. A designer first needs to act like an artist, drawing on his life experiences, collecting information, reading fashion

magazines, watching movies, etc. Then he must consolidate all the information before drawing the style to fit the physical features of a Chinese woman.

However, the report showed that when the economic system changed, designers isolated themselves from the market and the factories and created their designs behind closed doors. This made the design team, which was then called the technology research centre, a meaningless component. Lack of materials and market needs, a weak motivation system and the constraints of the economic system killed the design talents that had just sprouted in China.

Fashion: Back on Board

In 1979, the conclusion of the Third Plenum of the Eleventh Central Committee of the Communist Party of China marked a new era of the new China, which would step into a new reform period and open its doors again to the outside world. A remarkable fashion event in the same year was the fashion show presented by Monsieur Pierre Cardin in Beijing. To grant permission to an influential, world-class fashion designer to present a fashion show after the national catastrophe demonstrated the new government's firm commitment to its open-door policy. While the streets were full of grey and green uniforms, the show injected a fresh concept of modern clothes into the minds of Chinese people. After thirty years of the forbidden era, fashion was finally back on board again.

POST-MAO ERA: CONTEMPORARY CHINESE FASHION DESIGNERS
From Planned Economy to Market-oriented Economy

The Cultural Revolution had brought China nothing but a tremendous loss politically, economically, culturally and ideologically. Nearly thirty years of isolation from the world and the destruction of the national infrastructures and economic system made recovery slow and full of challenges. Until the 1980s, many people were still fearful of repercussions from the Cultural Revolution.

Economic reform is crucial in the development of industries and the lives of individuals. For many years, there was a harsh debate about China's economic reform: as a socialist country, should China switch to a market-oriented economic system and open its market to private businesses and foreign investors? Many people believed privately owned or foreigner-owned formats were the business models of capitalist countries, while socialism was supposed to be the equivalent of the central state-controlled model. In the 1980s few locations or industries were open to private or foreign investors. Most industries were still dominated by state-owned units and operated by a planned economic system, which in general meant competition was nonexistent. Suppliers, sellers, products and distribution methods were planned and controlled by the administration department of the state government.

At the end of 1992, the leader then, Deng Xiao-Ping, gave a famous speech in Shenzhen, a new developing city near Hong Kong. In his speech, he said that a market-oriented economic system and a planned economic system should not be the basis for differentiating between socialism and capitalism. Furthermore, he contended that China should execute a market-oriented economic system within a framework of socialist administration. The speech was influential due to its effect on China's later economic reform. In 1993, China explicitly announced its conversion to a market-oriented economic system, and since then, private business and foreign investments have boomed. Once again, the Chinese economy is favourable. With more money in hand and more freedom in spirit, people's lives were greatly changed as well: fashion was back, and shops once again had freedom and variety.

Improvement in the economic system motivated individuals to ambitiously develop private businesses. Most of the top private garment enterprises in China today were formed in the period after Deng's speech, and now they all play key roles in the local fashion industry and are strong backers in the development of local designers. At the same time, within the new economic framework, individual designers had the opportunity to build their own labels and business units. Most important, the new economic system increased the financial power of people and gave birth to a new generation of middle class and millionaires, a group of people who appreciate a designer's products and are therefore its major consumers.

Fashion Design Education in China

In the 1950s and 1960s the Central Academy of Arts & Design located in Beijing (now the Academy of Arts & Design, Tsing Hua University) organized training programs that focused on clothing design and production. Students were mostly professionals who worked in the garment industry. These training classes set the foundation for a full-time academic education later. In 1980 the same school started a three-year full-time apparel program. In 1982 it changed to a four-year educational program leading to a bachelor's degree. By the mid-1980s, Suzhou Institute of Silk Science, located on the east coast of China (now the Academy of Arts & Design, Suzhou University), Zhejiang Institute of Silk Science (now Zhejiang University of Science & Technology), Zhejiang Academy of Fine Arts (now China Academy of Fine Arts) in central east China, China Textile University (now Dong Hua University) in Shanghai, and Northwest Institute of Textile Engineering in Xi'an all stepped into the realm of apparel design.

When first established, the apparel courses were placed under the Department of Dying & Weaving, which was basically a textile design and engineering department. After gaining more experience and recruiting enough students, the schools separated the courses and established clothing design as an independent department.

The first wave of instructors was sourced from two camps: the arts and crafts departments of the schools, which taught fashion drawing and textile prints design, and tailors, who were in charge of the technical aspects of the course. Nobody was, in fact, a designer.

The origins of the instructors eventually determined the student recruitment method and education methodology of the school. Unlike most Western design schools, which view portfolios and conduct interviews to assess the design talents of students, Chinese students were recruited based on their portrait sketches and colour paintings, in addition to qualifications in common subjects. The exam format was no different than for those registering for fine arts schools, except for a lower entrance score for the arts part. Consequently, those who had a tailoring background but never learned drawing had little chance of passing the exam, while those who successfully passed the exams may not truly like fashion design. They registered for the design program because they loved drawing even though they were not good enough to pass the fine arts exam, or simply because they had no confidence in their ability to pass the exams of any other subjects. Since the entrance scores for clothing design programs were lower than for other programs, students found it easier to gain admission into college through the clothing design programs. These students usually took a three-month intensive painting program prior to the unified entrance exam. Their objective was to obtain a bachelor's degree rather than study fashion design. This exam format eventually proved an inappropriate way to select candidates for the programs.

Besides the common subjects which are compulsory components in China—Chinese literature, politics and economics, philosophy, and common English—in general, the four-year fashion design course teaches portrait sketching, colour painting, graphic design, principles of design, principles of colour, fashion illustration, design of fashion silhouette, accessory design, textile dying and prints, fashion psychology, fashion history and fabric science, with little time allocated to cutting and making.

Another course path, named Clothing Engineering, was created not long after the birth of Clothing Design. The course is geared towards a degree in science, so applicants take an exam in science and math skills instead of fine arts. It's another extreme end of the fashion curriculum; this pathway aims to provide students with skills in the cutting and making of clothing, and covers subjects like pattern cutting for women's wear, men's wear, and children's wear, technology of sewing and pressing, draping and modelling, computer aided design and fabric science, with little time allocated to fashion design.

The separation of 'drawing' courses and 'making' courses led to the isolation of the two camps—those who draw and belong to the 'arts camp', and those who make and belong to the 'tailors camp'. The two camps barely talk to each other. Students in arts camps feel superior to those in the tailors camps, while tailors think these so-called artists are just a bunch of people whose flat sketches can't be translated into real, three-dimensional garments.

The fashion design course is set-up similarly to a fashion illustration course. The creativity of fashion in general isn't covered, nor is inspiration research or creativity processing. Upon graduation, most students still have no concept of the three dimensions of clothing. Worse, many teachers are direct graduates of the same school and have little or no industrial background, which means the overall quality of the students doesn't meet the needs of the fashion industry. As China neared the twenty-first century, the gap between fashion design education and the needs of the real-world job market became more obvious and demonstrated the need for change. What fashion enterprises need are designers instead of artists or painters; they want designers who are able to work with a team of cutters, machinists, fabric sourcing specialists and marketers to transform the drawings into real clothes. More important, they want the clothes to sell and make money. The interaction between fashion schools in China and those overseas reinforces the shortcomings of local schools.

Fortunately, leading schools like China Academy of Fine Arts and Tsing Hua University are in the process of reforming their curricula. For instance, they invite visiting lecturers from industries that have more industrial background to teach the students, re-structure the curricula to balance the weight of arts and technology, add fashion marketing and management course pathways to meet the needs of the job market. Although the education program has been evolving, the core principles of the student recruitment and education system still remain. Even today, little has changed.

Nevertheless, the installation of clothing design courses still made great contributions to the development of Chinese fashion designers. Though there is room for improvement, the programs mark the official birth of professional fashion designers teams.

In 1994 the Raffles Education Corporation in Singapore established the first international fashion school in China. Most of its faculty are from the United States, Europe and Singapore. They demonstrated a totally fresh teaching and learning methodology to local fashion students. Students are not required to study Chinese literature, political economy and other subjects that are not related to the fashion business. Neither do students need to be good painters in order to be good designers. There is no entrance exam to get into the school, but the cost is extremely expensive. For a three-year fashion design program, tuition is seven times the local school tuition. The school is not qualified for accrediting degrees either, but promises to allow credit transfer to its counterparts in other countries. The school mostly attracted those who were fascinated by Western fashion and had strong financial support from their families. Due to its connection with the Western world, the school's name soon became well known in the industry and its graduates received good offers from local fashion companies.

The establishment of an international school broke the traditional methodology of teaching fashion in China. Subsequently, more international schools paraded into China and built joint programs with local fashion institutions.

From Garment Trade Fair to Fashion Week
Dalian International Fashion Festival

In August 1988, the municipal government of Dalian, a coastal city located in northeastern China, organized the Dalian Fashion Festival. For the first time, an event was aimed at promoting the concept of fashion as a lifestyle in China. Lasting eight days, it was composed of a trade fair, fashion show, fashion design contest and entertainment activities such as singing and dancing shows. The event attracted an audience of millions, and spread the concept of fashion lifestyle to ordinary people. The festival was renamed the Dalian International Fashion Festival three years later and extended its reach to include presenters and attendees from overseas. Despite being the oldest of any organized fashion festivals, it has become less influential today since macro cities such as Beijing and Shanghai began holding the same type of fashion event. Nevertheless, it pioneered the concept of Fashion City in an old oriental country that had just recovered from economic disaster, inspiring Beijing and Shanghai to follow suit.

China International Clothes and Accessory Fair

In May 1993 the China International Clothes and Accessory Fair (CHIC) was launched. It was organized by China Fashion Research Centre, China International Trading Centre, China Textile Importing & Exporting Company, and co-organized by France Association of Women's Wear and Men's Wear, the International Wool Bureau and Hong Kong Trading Bureau. The first fair invited the top three international fashion designers—Valentino Garavani, Gianfranco Ferre and Pierre Cardin— to present their collections. By end of the show, the three designers were honoured to meet with then-Chairman Jiang Ze-Ming.

Another achievement of the fair was the launching of one of the most influential fashion design contests in China, the Brother Cup International Young Fashion

Designer Contest. The contest was sponsored by the Japanese company that specialized in sewing machines, the Brother Group, which was the first enterprise to devote financial resources to support the discovery and development of young design talent. Wu Hai-Yan, one of the best-known and most prominent designers in China, was the first winner of the contest, which gained her national attention. The second year, the winner was Ma Ke, who later built the brand Exception, which is now widely regarded as the embodiment of the contemporary Chinese fashion designer brands. The Brother Cup was the first to present young designers as true stars. The Brother Cup and the China Cup, a contest organized by the Shanghai Fashion Festival, are the most influential fashion design contests in China today. Ten years later, in 2004, Hempel, one of the largest Chinese garment manufacturers and distributors, took over the sponsorship of the Brother Cup and renamed it the Hempel Cup International Young Fashion Designers Contest.

In 1995, CHIC started a new program intended to select the top ten Chinese fashion designers each year. The first time, selection was made through assessment of clothes, aspects of style, colours, use of fabric and accessories and workmanship, together with certified sales turnover of the past year and achievements of the nominees. The panel of judges came from the previously mentioned pioneering arts universities, which gave the whole process a strong academic flavour. In addition to the assessment from professional judges, the final list was also decided by vote from the public—in order to ensure the designer's popularity in the market. The first top ten fashion designers consisted of almost all the then-prominent names in the fashion industry in China. Four of them are interviewed in this book: Liu Yang, Ma Ke, Wang Xin-Yuan and Wu Hai-Yan.

The panel of judges now extends to entrepreneurs and media journalists. Some designers today criticize the fairness of the selection because the competition may be influenced by sponsors, and young but talented designers may not be able to participate because of lack of financial backing. Based on the rules, candidates for the top ten must come from the ranks of the exhibitors. Even so, being named one of the top ten fashion designers has been one of the key factors in evaluating the fame and achievements of designers in the industry.

The Golden Fashion Designer Award is the most prestigious honour that can be bestowed on local designers. The Golden Award is given to the number one designer selected from the top ten designers awards. Zhang Zhao-Da was the first winner.

The CHIC is one of the most prominent fashion fairs in Asia today. It demonstrates that China is switching its focus from exporting to servicing domestic markets and is transitioning from manufacturing to designing and branding. Today, the fair attracts more than 1,000 exhibitors from eighteen countries and more than 120,000 visitors from all over the world (www.chiconline.com.cn). To further extend its influence over the international markets, the fair is in the process of partnering with Pitti

Uomo in Florence, the most influential world-wide men's wear exhibition, and Who's Next in Paris, the well-known European showcase for creative and urban fashion.

Shanghai International Fashion Festival

In March 1995, following Beijing and Dalian, Shanghai kicked off the Shanghai International Fashion Festival. It serves as an international and local designers' show, offering seminars and a modelling contest, and features the influential China Cup Fashion Design Contest. Unlike the Brother Cup (now Hempel Cup) which stresses originality and innovation, the China Cup emphasizes the balance of creativity and wearability. Now the contest is divided into the categories of women's wear, men's wear, underwear and knitwear, and has attracted 30,000 candidates in the past ten years.

China Fashion Week

In 1997, with a spirit of brand, fashion and innovation in mind, China Fashion Week, an event totally engaged in promoting Chinese designers and designer brands, was born. To build its international image, China Fashion Week adopted the module of the international fashion week and organized the shows twice a year—spring and summer collection in March, and fall and winter collection in November. Unlike the other events which focus primarily on trade fairs and theatrical catwalk shows, China Fashion Week aims to be the trendsetter of the market, much like the four international fashion weeks in London, Milan, Paris and New York. Catwalk shows are no longer purely for theatrical purposes; they are presented to onlookers with a clear objective of commercial segmentation.

The awards reception is secondary to the seasonal collection show by designers and/or brands. Carried from CHIC, the Top Ten Fashion Designers Awards and Golden Fashion Designer Award are part of the programs of China Fashion Week now. In addition, China Fashion Week presents awards to outstanding fashion photographers, fashion editors, fashion models and fashion entrepreneurs in recognition of their noteworthy contributions to the design industry.

Targeted at students in fashion schools, the Firs New Talents Contest, the Wei Peng Jeans Design Contest and the San Bei Knitwear Design Contest (all sponsored by domestic garment enterprises) are other events which aim to motivate and promote new and young design talent in China.

Today, fashion fairs and fashion weeks are the platforms for designers and brands to show their work to the public. From trade fair to fashion week, from manufacturing centre to fashion and branding theme, the change of the theme marks the progress of the fashion industry in China—more international, more professional and more commercial.

Post-Mao Designers
1980s: Pioneering

After the end of the catastrophe of the Cultural Revolution, people were gradually pulled back to normal life. The cancellation of the Coupon System in 1984 finally liberated people's purchase power, but the overall economic market was still guided by a nationally planned monetary system. Many people still lacked the funds to satisfy their most basic needs, including enough simple clothes to wear. Having a nice piece of clothing was a luxury and very few people knew what clothing design was for and how it would affect their daily lives.

At the same time, both Pierre Cardin's fashion show in 1979 and Yves Saint Laurent's fashion exhibition in 1985 injected a new notion of clothing into the minds of Chinese people. To demonstrate the growing power of China to the world, the Ministry of Light Industry, then the administrator of the garment industry, sent a delegation to present ninety-four pieces of apparel at the Fiftieth International Women's Wear Trade Fair in Paris. This was the first time since the establishment of the new China that the world could greet the largest Asian country at an international fashion fair. In September 1987, Shanghai designer Chen Shan-Hua was sent to Paris together with eight Chinese fashion models. The group surprised the European audience with an enchanting fashion show in front of the Eiffel Tower. The announcement of Chen Shan-Hua's name at the show was a milestone for Chinese fashion designers. It was the first time a Chinese fashion designer took the spotlight at an influential international fashion event. The following day, 'Fashion from Mao's country' headlined newspapers around the world.

At the same time, the newly established fashion education system cultivated the first generation of post-Mao fashion designers. At the time, no one knew what these young design students would bring to the industry or how they would affect China's future fashions. Many of them eventually became pillars in the industry and contributed greatly to the development of the fashion business in China. Seven of the ten designers profiled in this book graduated from the pioneering fashion schools in China.

1990s: Practising

By the end of the 1980s thousands of design students had completed their academic education. Under the Planned Economic System, a governmental department matched graduating students to specific companies in specific locations. In principle, students were supposed to return to their hometowns, and they were usually dispatched to the state-owned garment enterprises in the local area. Unhappy with the management culture of the state-owned companies, some daring designers started businesses of their own. Inspired by the Western tradition, designers like Liu Yang, Wang Xin-Yuan and Ye Hong started their own design studios and labelled their products with their own names.

But life is always harder than expected. Although these young designers freed themselves from the state-owned cages, they found themselves in a world they didn't fully anticipate or understand. Building a successful fashion business is much more than just designing a collection. Insufficient financial resources to support the growth of their businesses, administrative policy constraints, immaturity of the overall consumer market, and most important, lack of business experience eventually forced most of these pioneers to abandon their dreams.

The emergence of these young designers and the increasing competition in the garment industry caught the attention of local entrepreneurs. Adventurous businessmen foresaw the opportunity to take advantage of the fame of these promising designers to increase the added value of their products. In the mid-1990s, the export business was under immense pressure from price competition, quota limits and constant trade barriers. Additionally, the domestic market was under serious attack from imported international brands. Local fashion companies could do nothing to fight back except copy the products and offer them at a lower price, though this left little profit for the companies. The Chinese entrepreneurs could not understand how a product labelled with an international brand name costing only US$5.00 to manufacture could be sold for US$50.00 once exported to overseas countries. If the same product was labelled without a branded name, the selling price dropped dramatically. The group of entrepreneurs finally realized that Chinese companies had been selling *products* instead of *brands*. Having brand equity is key to the financial success and sustainability of an enterprise. Consequently, these Chinese manufacturers changed course and switched to a branding strategy. They realized they needed designers who could lead the development of new products and increase the added value of their products in the market.

In 1996, Firs, then the largest men's suit manufacturer in China, put out a national recruitment advertising for a chief designer, offering annual compensation of one million Ren Min Bi (RMB). At that time, the average salary per year in urban cities like Shanghai and Beijing was around 10,000 RMB or even less. The offer broke all records for designer compensation and started the marriage trend between fashion companies and designers. Wang Xin-Yuan and Zhang Zhao-Da eventually became the successors to the original position. The trend was continued by the brand Younger with Liu Yang, and China Fashion Group with Wu Hai-Yan. The position of fashion designers was elevated overnight as were the number of applicants to fashion design schools. People believed that being a fashion designer would advance them to star-like status in China just like it is in Europe.

Like marriage in real life, marriage between designers and companies was not always sanguine. Neither designers nor entrepreneurs had experience of the duo partnership. Entrepreneurs expected to use designers to improve the brand values, and eventually the sales turnover. Designers wished to prove their value to businesses. It seemed as if they shared the same goal, but they did not speak the same language. A common issue was that before products hit the retail floor, designers were required to present their work to company managers for approval. Managers believed they knew what would sell and what would not. Designers were often asked to change some of the design elements—the collar or neckline, the sleeves or buttons—even though the final look of the products may be completely different from the original design and may be unattractive in the eye of the designer. As businessmen, entrepreneurs pursue profit. Ensuring that the products created by their designers will eventually make money is vital to the survival of the company.

Tension between the enterprises and the designers created controversy. The designers were accused of spending money without capturing enough market shares for the companies. Some detractors even commented that these designers just wanted to fill their own pockets with cash without regard for the success of the company. The entrepreneurs spent a lot of money to promote the designers through fashion shows and events; these designers were considered famous in the Chinese fashion industry, yet they had few fans in the consumer market. Their fame did not extend to ordinary people, hence no one was seen as a fashion trendsetter who could create commercial value for their company.

With both sides feeling as if all creative alternatives had been exhausted, the majority of the designer/company marriages spiralled apart. Though regarded generally as a failure, the marriage experience proved to be a lesson to both entrepreneurs and designers. On reflection, the entrepreneurs recognized that their over-interference with the designers severely hurt the designers' confidence and sense of innovation, which then reduced the value of employing creative designers. At the same time, the designers learned that to be successful, one must be both a creative artist and a skilful marketer—or alternatively with a partner who has strong marketing sense. Being the best designer in the country doesn't mean much if you can't stay in business.

Twenty-first Century: Proliferating

The approach of the new century also brought fortunes to China. Joining the World Trade Organization in 2001, winning the right in 2001 to host the 2008 Olympic Games, sending its first manned spacecraft into orbit in 2003 and the growing GDP at two digits per year, all helped China to begin accelerating its position in the world. Its relatively peaceful political environment and relaxed economic policy attracted foreign investments more than ever. In the fashion business, high-end international brands flooded Chinese markets and opened shops in macro urban cities. Many people believed that China would become the largest market for luxury goods consumption in the near future.

The opening of the country's borders provided more opportunities to Chinese fashion designers to see the world outside China and broaden their views in both design and brand building. Though generally considered a failure in business in the 1990s, the first generation of post-Mao designers not only pioneered a market for local designer brands, but also contributed greatly to the education of a younger generation. Most of them shy away from the spotlight today, but some are still occasionally seen in the media. Liu Yang, Wang Xin-Yuan, Wu Hai-Yan and Zhang Zhao-Da, the four most prominent designers of this era, are either partnering with enterprises or devoting their time and talent to fashion institutions such as schools and industrial associations. At the same time, the younger generation of designers born in the late 1960s or early 1970s is now emerging in the Chinese market. Compared with the first generation, the younger ones are more grounded and are taking solid steps in building their own brands. Examples include Ma Ke with her Exception line, Liang Zi with her brand TangY and Wang Yi-Yang with his line Zuczug. They have the potential of becoming the mainstay of local designer brands. Those in the next wave, born in the 1980s, are widely envisioned as the future of Chinese fashion design. Although still very young and inexperienced, with the growing trend of globalization and supported by the ascending power of the nation, their vigour and unconstrained spirits allow them to be more innovative than their predecessors. Who knows? Some of them may represent the zeitgeists in the fashion world of the future.

2 THE 1980s: THE FIRST GENERATION—PIONEERS

BACKGROUND
SOCIO-ECONOMIC CONDITIONS

In the 1980s, although the general economy was dominated by state-owned enterprises, the open-door policy encouraged people to be self-employed, or partner with other people and form a collective firm. However, the idea of the state-owned enterprise as a life-long job had been fixed in people's minds. Because the state-owned enterprises normally retain people until their retirement, few cared to abandon a very stable job, although it paid only meagre wages. Therefore, the first generation of self-employed people mostly consisted of those from the countryside who had no jobs anyway, or those released from jails, whom nobody wanted to hire. Nobody expected that these grass-roots people would someday become one of the richest groups of people. By vending clothes, fruits, and other goods, many owners of today's clothing companies were self-employed at first. But in general, the state was still vigilant about the development of the economy because of concerns over capitalism, widely considered to be the antagonist of the socialism system at the time.

In 1983 Hu Yao-Bang, the then-secretary-general, encouraged the clothing companies to make 'more beautiful' clothes for Chinese people, and he was one of the first to wear Western suits in public as a sign of the open-door policy. In 1986, at the Seventh Congress of the Communist Party, the Seventh National Five-year Plan included the making of clothing as a plan to develop industry. With this policy, China jumped to the fore as the largest garment producer and exporter world-wide in 1994.

THE CLOTHING INDUSTRY

The clothing industry in China in the 1980s had little sense of the concepts of 'fashion', 'designer' and 'brand'. Chinese people at the time bought clothes mostly for functional needs. Information on trends was still very limited, but better than it was in the 1960s and 1970s. People absorbed trend information from the fashion (clothing) magazines and movies. Popular wear included stretch leg-hugging denims, boot-cut denims, bat-wing sweaters, leather jackets, Western suits, and A-line knee-length skirts. Some trendy women wore mini-skirts. Although there was more diversity in style, most people still adhered to the style of the 1970s.

An article headlined 'Clean the Spiritual Contamination vs. Beautify Life' (*Wuran bixu Qingchu, Shenghuo yao meihua*) published in *The China Youth Daily* (*Zhongguo Qingnian Bao*) on 17 November 1983 depicted how this affected the ideology of people in the early 1980s.

> There is something emerging in a few places that some of our comrades accused young ladies of perming their hair and putting on Snowflake cream [*Xuehua Gao* in Chinese, a famous skin-care product at the time]. These comrades interfere with young people wearing stylish clothes and forbid young people to play the social dancing…These comrades marked such a lifestyle as belonging to the 'bourgeois classes', and regarded such phenomena as 'spiritual contamination' and are strongly opposed to it. It deserves our attention that these comrades confused young people's wish to beautify their lives with 'spiritual contamination'…
> (Xu 1983: 1)

It was reported that in order to prevent the youth from being 'spiritually contaminated', extreme measures were taken. For instance, any pictures with a woman in an off-shoulder dress, a gymnast on the high-low bar or even a naked baby were regarded as *yellow images* ('pornography' in Chinese). Anybody with shoulder-length curly hair and boot-cut pants was not permitted in the schools and factories.

Fortunately such extreme ideology did not stop people from the pursuit of beauty. The senior management of the State Council underlined its determination to open the door by inviting famous designers from Europe to China.

Pierre Cardin was the first person to bring the concept of fashion—and fashion models—to China after the post-Mao era, and as such, his name is preeminent when speaking of Chinese fashion history. He conducted the first international fashion show for the Chinese in 1979, although at the time the audience was restricted to professionals. His second show in 1981, in the Beijing Hotel, was open to the public. Other international designers that should not be forgotten are Yves Saint Laurent, who exhibited his exquisite artefacts in the China National Museum of Fine Arts in 1985, and Junka Kashino, who paraded her fashions in China in the Beijing Hotel in the same year.

Fashion Models

Influenced by Pierre Cardin's show, and with the support of his assistant Song Huai-Jia—one of the contributors to the development of Chinese fashion—the state-owned Shanghai Garment Company formed the first Chinese fashion model performance team in 1980. The first models were picked from female workers in textile factories; the basic requirements were 'female, 1.64m in height, 80 cm/60 cm/80 cm in the bust/waist/hips'.

Unlike the model agency system in Western countries, the Chinese fashion models worked full-time for the company—the same as in any other profession. The models were paid minimum wage, plus commissions from each show.

In the 1980s, 'fashion model' was a new term to the Chinese. In the eyes of most, pretty women displaying their bodies in different postures on the stage was equivalent to coquetry, which was considered shameful and caused strong objections from the parents of these young models. To see their daughters wear strapless or off-shoulder dresses was like seeing them parade naked in public. Therefore, models were only permitted to wear clothes that covered their bodies properly.

Model shows at the very beginning were limited to professionals, basically traders from overseas and Chinese officials. The shows became open to the public a few years later, but mainly as entertainment, like dancing or acrobatic performances. Shows were mostly seen in nightclubs or restaurants.

In 1986 model Shi Kai attended an international model contest and received a special prize for being the first Chinese model to appear in an international contest. In 1989, the city of Shanghai hosted the Xunda Cup Fashion Model Contest, the first fashion model contest in post-Mao China.

Fashion Magazines

In 1980 the first fashion magazine, *Fashion* (*Shizhuang*), was created, focusing primarily on tailoring techniques. In 1988 the first international fashion magazine, *Elle*, was introduced to the Chinese.

Fashion Trade Fairs

The first clothing trade fair in post-Mao China, the National New Style Clothing Trade Fair (*Quanguo Xinhaoxing Fuzhuang Zhanlanhui*), was held in 1981 in Beijing. The first trend forecasting show in new China was held in 1986 in the People's Great Hall in Beijing.

The first fashion week in new China was held in August 1988 in Dalian, Liaoning Province. At the time, it was called the Dalian Fashion Festival, later changed to the Dalian International Fashion Festival.

The Industrial Association

The first clothing association—Beijing Clothing Association—was established in October 1984.

Fashion Design Contest

The first officially acknowledged national fashion design contest was the Gold Scissors Contest, in November 1985.

Exposure Overseas

The first exposure to fashion fairs in the Western world post-Mao was in September 1985. The Chinese team attended the Fiftieth International Women's Wear Trade Fair in Paris.

The first Chinese fashion designer exposure to the audience in the West post-Mao was in September 1987. The Shanghai designer, Chen Shan-Hua, attended the Second Paris International Fashion Festival and received applause from the European media. The show was headlined 'Fashion from Mao's Country'.

Fashion Education

In 1980, the Central Academy of Arts and Design (now the Tsing-Hua University of Fine Arts) offered a three-year program of clothing design. In 1982, it initiated the first clothing design course leading to a bachelor's degree.

May 1988 saw the establishment of the Beijing Fashion Institute, the first professional fashion institute in China.

Fashion Designers

The first generation of fashion designers post-Mao mostly came from the graduates of the schools. And they became famous overnight through various design contests. In the 1980s, fashion design contests were probably the only short-cut for a designer to become well known. The various fashion trade shows and fashion festivals were used to accelerate the fame of designers. But their fame was generally short-lived. New designers' names were seen in newspapers and magazines, but a few months or one year later, the same names were rarely seen.

Because the national economy was dominated by the state-owned enterprises, most designers went to the state-owned companies and worked as either apprentices or clothing designers. But as little creativity was required, they spent their time on copying pictures from magazines, or following the instructions from traders and providing manufacturing service to overseas buyers.

Some pioneers took the initiative and launched their own brands in the 1980s, but few survived. The stories of the following four designers—Wang Xin-Yuan,

Wu Hai-Yan, Frankie Xie, Liu Yang—illustrate the growth experience of the first generation.

WANG XIN-YUAN: A GENERAL IN THE REALM OF FASHION

Unlike most contemporary designers who dress themselves in outrageous ways to identify themselves as a designer, Xin-Yuan is always seen in immaculate business attire or a smart casual pull-over jersey top mixed with straight-cut trousers. Of the designers interviewed, Xin-Yuan looks least like a designer in appearance; both his mien and demeanour make him more like a gentleman than a designer. When asked the reason, he replied that because he holds several different roles, including General Manager and Chief Designer, he often receives different types of people each day, including journalists, government officials, entrepreneurs, professors and students. It would be inappropriate to be dressed like a rock star with holes in his clothes and piercings in his ears and nose.

All Xin-Yuan's friends know that General Patton is his idol, and his admiration of General Patton adds to his uniqueness as a designer. He is artistic, sensitive,

Figure 2.1 Wang Xin-Yuan and Pierre Cardin, 1986.
Photographer: Liu Yang.

affectionate and discerning, and these traits are intertwined with his Patton-like qualities: talented, ambitious, determined, tough, arrogant and demanding.

PORTFOLIO

Born: in a small village in Zhejiang province in 1958. Now based in the city of Shanghai.

Education: Graduated with a bachelor's degree in Clothing Design from Suzhou Institute of Silk Science, 1985.

Career: Dispatched to a rural village under the Rustication Movement, 1974; served in the Army 1976–1981; worked for the Beijing Silk Factory as a designer, 1985; moved to *Fashion,* the first fashion magazine in new China, and was responsible for fashion events, 1986; arts director for fashion shows presented at the Sixtieth Guangzhou Trade Fair, the largest trade fair in China, 1986; writer and editor for the TV documentary program *Fashion Culture* for CCTV (China Central TV), the only authorized national TV channel in China; trained at the Hong Kong Institute of Fashion Design, at the same time worked in the Hong Kong JMT fashion firm as a designer, 1987–1989; chief designer for the first private fashion label in new China, *Yin Meng* ('Silver Dream'), 1989–1991; first to launch office wear specifically designed for Chinese businesswomen, 1990; built own fashion house—Xin Yuan Fashion Company Limited, 1992–1996; together with another fashion icon, Zhang Zhao-Da, the duo were recruited to be the chief designers for Firs, a women's label funded by the Shanshan Garment Group, then the largest men's suit manufacturer, 1996–1999; built Galaxy Model Agency with his fashion model friend, 2000–present; appointed Secretary General of Shanghai International Fashion Federation, 2006–present.

Selected Awards and Achievements

1987, second-place winner of Hong Kong Young Designers Contest

1988, third-place winner of Fashion Designers contest organized by Shenzhen Fashion Festival

1990, the first designer to launch office wear specifically designed for Chinese businesswomen

1993, 1994, Famous Label Award by CHIC

1995, Top Ten Chinese Fashion Designers Award by CHIC

1997, Outstanding Chinese Fashion Designers Award by UNESCO

Selected Commentary from the Media

Since Wang launched it last year, the Sinyuan label has been favoured by young Chinese career women. (Mao 1992: 4)

The 'Not Me, but the Wind' Wang Xin-Yuan and Zhang Zhao-Da Ready-to-Wear Show is making record-breaking history…after a debut in Beijing, the Shanshan Group invested another 10 million to deliver the show to another 15 cities…(Qi 1998: 6)

Wang Xin-Yuan is the standard-bearer in the regime of fashion shows, largely attributed to his superior skills in directing mega-scale fashion shows that span time and space. He certainly deserves the title of number one. (Gu 2000: 10)

The Great Wall fashion show was a remarkable event for Wang and Chinese fashion designers as a whole. For starters, it was the first time that a modern fashion show was held on the Great Wall, a symbol of the country's glorious history. (Li 2000: 10)

BIOGRAPHY
A Peasant, Soldier and Painter (1958–1981)

Born in a small town in Zhejiang Province in 1958, Xin-Yuan has had many different jobs in his life, just like everyone else of his generation. The name *Xin-Yuan*, which means 'new century', was given to him because he was born on 1 January. But the lucky-sounding date did not guarantee good fortune for him. By the time he was born, China was in the Great Leap Forward[1], a movement that aimed to increase China's economic power in a short time in order to surpass the Western countries. This was done by exaggerating the capacity and capability of the Chinese people. This movement was followed by the Three Years of Natural Catastrophe[2] which in fact was a result of the debilitated national economic infrastructure. After completing his intermittent education in preliminary and high school during the Cultural Revolution, Xin-Yuan was then dispatched to a rural area to live and farm with local peasants under the Rustication Movement. After two years of farming life, at the age of eighteen, Xin-Yuan was conscripted into the army and served in an artillery regiment.

Xin-Yuan had loved to paint ever since he was a little boy. As a child, he often copied the ubiquitous portraits of Chairman Mao. When riding his bicycle and passing by the portraits that hung everywhere during the Cultural Revolution, Xin-Yuan always stopped to see which portraits most resembled the great Chinese leader. When he was in high school, his painting teacher noticed his enthusiasm and talent for drawing and became the first teacher to lead him into the elegant world of fine arts.

Figure 2.2 Wang Xin-Yuan in the Military Uniform, 1980.
Image courtesy of Wang Xin-Yuan.

When he graduated from high school at sixteen, Xin-Yuan was dispatched to a small village in the province near his hometown under the Rustication Movement. Though planting every day in the field, Xin-Yuan retained his enthusiasm for the arts and practised his drawing skills daily by painting on the abandoned walls in his spare time. His passion for painting eventually brought him to the attention of the conscription personnel. They accidentally found a piece of an oil-painting from an abandoned wall, one of the masterpieces created by Xin-Yuan. The painting, depicting a scene from a well-known story about a famous Chinese battle, is a eulogy to the army of the Chinese Communist Party. At one time, Xin-Yuan's father was the head of a marine fleet and that made Xin-Yuan very comfortable around those in military uniform. When asked if he would like to serve in the army, Xin-Yuan excitedly accepted the offer. Ambitious Xin-Yuan swore in front of his friends that he would not come back to see them until he had been promoted to the four-pocket-uniform, the icon of officers. (Soldiers' uniforms had only two pockets.) During his military service, Xin-Yuan was responsible for propaganda and his painting skill once again made him a star in the army.

While he enjoyed painting, Xin-Yuan found himself still in the two-pocket uniform after four years. Feeling disappointed that he had not achieved his desired rank, he made the biggest decision of his life—to go back to school and continue his study of the arts.

First-generation Fashion Design Student (1981–1985)

Xin-Yuan was nearly twenty-four when he made up his mind to go to college. By then, it had been more than seven years since he had left high school. The short restoration of the unified entrance exam to college since the Cultural Revolution reinforced the overall competition of the exam; numerous young people wanted to attend colleges to make up the education time missed during the Cultural Revolution. During the six months of preparation for the exam, Xin-Yuan spent all his spare time studying and drawing. Fortunately, his painstaking work was rewarded with an offer letter from Suzhou Institute of Silk Science, one of the oldest silk textile institutes in China.

Upon entry to the institute, Xin-Yuan registered for a course called Dying and Weaving. He took three years of textile design in the college. In the fourth year, the school added a design pathway under the course of Dying and Weaving. Xin-Yuan and his classmates—approximately twenty students—were split into two groups: the students seated on the left side of the classroom were to study clothing design, and the students on the right side were to learn interior design. At the time, none of the students knew exactly what clothing design and interior design were all about. Xin-Yuan's destiny was sealed; he sat on the left side of the classroom and, therefore, was categorized into clothing design.

With the genes of a general in his blood, Xin-Yuan was a top student in almost all aspects, including the design courses, sports, dancing and writing. At the same time, he was the monitor of the class, the head of the school's Students' Union, and a protégé of all the teachers. However, when he graduated, his excellent school record did not result in the job that he had dreamed of. Under the Planned Economic System, students did not have the means or opportunity to look for jobs by themselves, as the government matched jobs for all graduated students. Every year Xin-Yuan's school allowed one student to be sent to Hong Kong to work. Prior to 1997, Hong Kong was the equivalent of going abroad to those living on the mainland. Like many other young people, Xin-Yuan had dreamt of working in Hong Kong for a long time. He did not expect that he would eventually have to attribute his losing the opportunity to go to Hong Kong to his excellent school record; his school wanted to keep this outstanding student in the college and train him to be a lecturer and eventually a professor. When Xin-Yuan was informed about this decision, he found himself with only two options: stay in school to start his academic career, or go to a state-owned manufacturer in Beijing—Beijing Silk Factory.

Xin-Yuan chose to go to Beijing—a city where he had no friends, no family and nothing that belonged to him.

A Designer in a State-owned Enterprise (1985–1989)

Xin-Yuan was the first fashion designer assigned to Beijing Silk Factory. No one knew exactly what the young designer could do for the textile miller when he registered in the state-owned factory. After being assigned five dressmakers and a small, gloomy loft as his working space, Xin-Yuan never received any instruction about his work. Out of necessity he took the lead in his clothing design and guided his five dressmakers as they produced samples based on his sketches. His other duties included making clothes for his colleagues in other departments as a favour to them. This drab life fuelled his ambition day after day, even as it severely hurt his self-esteem. Then a group of famous fashion models from Shanghai came to the factory. Since the models were renting Beijing Silk Factory for their rehearsal site, Xin-Yuan took his designs and went to see the leader of the group to ask her if the models could try on the clothes he'd designed. He received a devastating answer. The leader told Xin-Yuan in no uncertain terms that these models were the top models in China and they would never wear clothes designed by an ordinary person. Clutching his designs, an embarrassed Xin-Yuan went back to the office. Upset and anguished, he swore that one day these top models would wear clothes designed by Wang Xin-Yuan.

One year later, *Fashion,* the earliest state-run fashion magazine house in China, recruited Xin-Yuan from Beijing Silk Factory when the head of the magazine noticed Xin-Yuan's talent from his graduation work when they visited Suzhou Institute of Silk Science. Xin-Yuan then started his career as a fashion journalist. At the magazine, Xin-Yuan was primarily responsible for organizing fashion events. Right after his arrival in 1986 he was challenged with organizing thirteen fashion shows at the Sixtieth Chinese Export Commodities Fair in Guangzhou, the oldest and largest exporting trade fair in China. Xin-Yuan seemed to have a flair for knowing how to organize big events like fashion shows, and the success of the shows finally brought him to another turning point in his life.

In 1987, *Fashion* magazine decided to send four young designers to Hong Kong for further fashion design training. Sponsored by the magazine's business partner in Hong Kong, Xin-Yuan and three other young designers were sent to the Hong Kong Institute of Fashion to study. Since the local people there spoke Cantonese instead of Mandarin Chinese, a totally different dialect, Xin-Yuan could understand nothing and had to guess what the teachers were talking about in class. But from the students who were sitting in the same room with him he learned the so-called institute was actually more the equivalent of a night school that taught housewives to make clothes. Three months later, when he could finally understand the local dialect, he decided to abandon his studies and look for a job.

While he was job hunting, he noticed a news article in the local newspaper about the Second Hong Kong Young Fashion Designers' Contest. He and his three colleagues from Mainland China entered different categories of the contest and sent in their design works individually. Three out of the four won prizes, and Xin-Yuan won second prize in the evening dress category. It was the first time Mainland Chinese fashion designers received awards overseas, and they attracted a lot of attention from the local media. Xin-Yuan's confidence in his design talent was rejuvenated.

While doing part-time painting work for a local fine arts studio, a friend introduced Xin-Yuan to a local fashion entrepreneur who was then the owner of one of the

Figure 2.3 Wang Xin-Yuan and his design piece at the Second
Hong Kong Young Fashion Designers' Contest, 1987.
Image courtesy of Wang Xin-Yuan.

well-known local fashion labels in Hong Kong—the JMT Fashion Company. By co-incidence, the owner, Mr. Xu, was one of the members of the judging panel for the Second Hong Kong Young Fashion Designers' Contest. It seemed like a gift from God. Mr. Xu recognized Xin-Yuan and immediately offered him a position in his company.

Thus, two years after graduation from school, Xin-Yuan finally began fashion design in earnest. He started as a junior designer making 1,500 Hong Kong dollars (HK\$). A few months later, in 1987, he was promoted and became responsible for all clothing and visual image design for the company and his income was increased to 12,000 HK\$ per month, commensurate with his performance. Compared to the average wage of 50 RMB per month in Mainland China, it was a huge amount of money to Xin-Yuan.

Xin-Yuan wanted to stay in Hong Kong longer so that he could gain more experience from the local fashion market before returning to his country. But his plan was interrupted by an outrageous set of circumstances.

In 1988, encouraged by his friends on the mainland, Xin-Yuan decided to attend the Shenzhen Fashion Designers Contest. Shenzhen, located in the south of Mainland China, one hour away from Hong Kong by train, was one of the earliest special economic zones opened to foreign investors in 1980. Financially supported by the JMT company, Xin-Yuan's design work was included in the final selected list and was therefore eligible for the finals of the contest. Back in the 1980s, Hong Kong was still administrated by the British government and all Mainland Chinese were required to apply for a visa to get into Hong Kong. Xin-Yuan got a single-entry visa into Hong Kong, which meant if he wanted to go to Shenzhen for the final design contest, he would need another visa to go back to Hong Kong. With help from his friends he succeeded in getting another visa and went to Shenzhen, and successfully received his prize from the contest.

After returning to Hong Kong, he was dismayed when *Fashion* magazine recalled him to Beijing. Somehow the news that Xin-Yuan went to Shenzhen for a contest was leaked to the head of the magazine. This was a problem because in the 1980s and early 1990s anyone who was dispatched abroad either for business or study by a state-owned company or state-controlled administrative and/or business unit would need a political background scrutiny from the government. This was to ensure that the person would not do anything that might undermine the security of the country, and also that the person wouldn't sneak into any other countries (in fact, in the 1980s a lot of Chinese people slipped from the control of the companies that sent them abroad and 'disappeared'). Therefore, most companies requested that their overseas staff submit a report for travel approval before taking an absence from their workplace.

Xin-Yuan had not informed his Beijing home office before he went to Shenzhen for the contest. Obviously he was aware of the policy; in fact, he once refused to go to Europe for a fashion market tour with his boss Mr. Xu for this reason. However, he never expected that to return to his home country one time he would need sanction as well. Because he neglected to inform his home office that he was going to

Shenzhen, he was unexpectedly charged with the offence of 'decamping abroad'. Xin-Yuan had to stop working and studying in Hong Kong and return to Beijing. In the home office, the powers-that-be demanded that Xin-Yuan write a confession letter that would be submitted to a peer group for review. He refused to write the report, saying he never meant to leave his country and decamp elsewhere. Even today when he recalls the story, he still does not understand how returning to his hometown could be construed as 'decamping abroad'.

Xin-Yuan's experience was a vivid illustration of the isolated life of Chinese designers in the early phase of the reform of 1980s China. After the Shenzhen incident, Xin-Yuan reverted to normal fashion design work. Learning from his experience in Hong Kong, Xin-Yuan proposed to the leaders of the magazine a plan to host the first fashion model contest in China. At the time, such a contest required sanctions from four different ministries of the state—the Ministry of Culture, the Ministry of Textiles, the Ministry of Trading and the Ministry of Commerce. Xin-Yuan took advantage of his social network and successfully received the four stamps from the four departments, which were in the quintessential Chinese format, signifying that the stamp holder was 'authorized'.

Because it was the first fashion model contest in China, the event soon made the news, drawing the scrutiny of the State Council, which in turn summoned Xin-Yuan to Zhong Nanhai, the equivalent of the United States' White House and Britain's No. 10 Downing Street. While at Zhong Nanhai, Xin-Yuan was told he had to stop the fashion model contest because at the time the Chinese-Vietnam war was going on and it was not an appropriate time to host a beauty contest. Xin-Yuan tried his best to explain that it was not a beauty contest, but to no avail. He finally had to abandon his aggressive plan of hosting the fashion model contest in China. One year later, in 1989, another man—Zhang Jian—successfully launched the first fashion model contest in China.

These two incidents eroded Xin-Yuan's passion to work for the state-owned companies, and in the beginning of the 1990s, he noticed the emerging power of private companies in the fashion industry. One day, a young man knocked on his door and asked Xin-Yuan if he would like to join a private company called *Yin Meng* (Silver Dream).

Working for One of the First Private Fashion Labels in New China—Yin Meng (1990)

Yin Meng, one of the first private fashion labels in new China, was founded by two young men in Beijing in the late 1980s. By the time Xin-Yuan joined the company, *Yin Meng* had attained local market awareness. The two young men invited Xin-Yuan to join them because the company was in a growing phase and they needed someone like Xin-Yuan who was skilled in fashion design.

Xin-Yuan added a new concept to the label's products when he observed the emergence of modern Chinese businesswomen. Unlike older Chinese women, who were mostly illiterate manual labour workers, these modern women were well-educated office workers with good incomes. This particular group of women was later called *white collar,* a term that was widely believed to be the name used by bourgeoisie countries at the time, so he replaced 'white collar' with the name 'professionals'.

Xin-Yuan noticed businesswomen in Hong Kong were always dressed in immaculate executive suits, while most Chinese businesswomen seemed to have no appropriate business attire. Wherever they were—at home, shopping, travelling—they always wore the same types of clothes. Xin-Yuan took advantage of this opportunity and decided to bridge the gap by providing stylish office attire for these female professionals.

The new product launching was successful and sales soared. However, as the company became more profitable, the three partners could not agree on how to split the profits. It was a hard lesson learned, something that should have been decided upon at the beginning.

Savvy businessmen forge an agreement about shares before starting a new venture. However, in the early 1990s, when the national Chinese economy was still mostly influenced by the Planned Economic System, it wasn't surprising that three inexperienced young men did not understand the notion of shareholders. The ego-centric nature of humans dictated their decisions, overriding rationality; hence, they could not reach a consensus on the profit sharing. When Xin-Yuan recounted the story, he concluded that no one was in fact wrong; their inability to come to an agreement should be attributed to their youth and lack of experience. The result probably could have been turned around if they had been led by an older, more experienced manager.

Creating the Designer Label of Sinyuan (1992–1996)

In 1992, Xin-Yuan left *Yin Meng* and started a business of his own. Jointly funded with the aforementioned Mr. Xu, a benevolent man, Xin-Yuan took the dual roles of General Manager and Chief Designer in the company. He continued to strive for a market position of office wear for Chinese businesswomen in his new label Sinyuan. The business did well from the start; Xin-Yuan soon opened two boutiques on the main streets of Beijing, as well as in local mainstream department stores.

Xin-Yuan's dream of being a General Manager had finally come true. While venturing into a fashion empire of his own, Xin-Yuan also attained a great deal of fame in the fashion world through the success of his business. The Xin-Yuan label was the consecutive winner of Golden Awards of CHIC from 1993 to 1995. In 1995, he was a winner in the first Top Ten Fashion Designers contest in China. In the 1990s, Xin-Yuan obtained a great deal of public exposure for the launch of his new collections through fashion shows, as a judge for all sorts of fashion designer and modelling contests, as a presenter of fashion culture programs on TV, and as a columnist for a fashion journal.

However, problems often accompany good fortune. Not long after launching his new collection, Xin-Yuan found his products being chased by followers and copyists. Overnight, his office attire designs became all the rage in the city, and all the shops in Beijing were packed with similar styles of business wear for women. Worse, his work finally revealed the inequality between his weakness as a General Manager and his strength as a Chief Designer. Playing these dual roles presented him with a double dilemma: he had to spend most of his time on managing the company, both internally and externally, giving him little time to design. Overall, he proved himself a good designer but not a successful businessman. Four years after the company was established, Xin-Yuan's sales turnover was stagnant and his office expenses were escalating.

The increasing market competition together with the complexity of playing dual roles in his company pushed Xin-Yuan into a corner. It was time for a new journey.

Figure 2.4 The shop frontage of Sinyuan brand, early 1990s.
Image courtesy of Wang Xin-Yuan.

Figure 2.5 The fashion show of Sinyuan brand, 1991.
Photographer: Zhang Ya-Jian.

Chief Designer of Firs (1997–1999)

By the end of 1996, a recruitment ad for Chief Fashion Designer at the Shanshan Group attracted a great deal of attention from the fashion industry. The position offered a remuneration of 1 million RMB per year. At the time, the average income in urban cities like Shanghai and Beijing was no more than 10,000 RMB per year. The advertisement eventually led to an increase in the number of students who enrolled in fashion design programs in following years. These students regarded the advertisement as a signal that promoted the overall status of fashion designers, who in the past had been looked down on as being the equivalent of tailors.

Shanshan is a pioneer in the garment industry in China. It was the first clothing manufacturer to build the largest distribution channel network in China, the first to import the concept of CIS (Corporate Image System), and in 1996 it became the first IPO apparel enterprise in China. Its manufacturing system was considered first class.

Its leader, Zheng Yong-Gang, was an influential reformer in the garment industry in China. As a matter of fact, the recruitment ad was more for the purpose of commerce than for recruitment. Before running the ad, Zheng had already reached

Figure 2.6 Product line of Sinyuan brand.
Photographer: Wang Xin-Yuan.

Figure 2.7 Product line of Sinyuan brand.
Photographer: Wang Xin-Yuan.

Figure 2.8 Product line of Sinyuan brand.
Photographer: Wang Xin-Yuan.

Figure 2.9 Product line of Sinyuan brand.
Photographer: Wang Xin-Yuan.

an agreement with the two top designers in China—Wang Xin-Yuan and Zhang Zhao-Da—who would jointly assume the position of chief designers for Firs.

The ad raised the income bar for fashion designers, and without a doubt also raised the awareness of Firs and its two new chief designers. With stronger financial backing from Firs, the designing duo started a 'new century' for Chinese fashion designers.

The duo was to create a new women's brand called Firs for Shanshan, which only designed men's suits at the time. Firs's goal was to be the number-one couture brand for Chinese women.

To create the image of a truly haute couture fashion house, the pair first spent US$140,000 to put out the most expensive fashion catalogue in the history of China. The photo shoot was produced by people from a diverse international background. Two top-class Chinese fashion models, Chen Juan-Hong and Ma Yan-Li, starred in the catalogue. The photographer, who had shot for the magazine *Face* and the brand Prada, was invited from Europe, and the French stylist and art director from Hong Kong. The shooting took place in a castle in Paris at the cost of US$10,000 per day.

Right after the expensive catalogue shoot, the design duo moved into the next phase: extravagant, large-scale fashion shows throughout China. The first show, named 'Into the Sphere of Oriental', included the sixty top Chinese models, rented the most luxurious hotel in China at the time, Beijing Tian Lun Hotel, and was one of the major fashion events in China in 1997. The design and production of the clothes for the show followed the haute couture production standard. All the clothes were first fitted to the models in toile then finished in sumptuous, imported fabrics. To increase the company's market accessibility, the design of the clothes aimed for an overall balance of aesthetics and wearability, a subtle and unexaggerated look. The show adopted the format of a theatrical performance. It displayed a chronological evolution of oriental women's fashions, from women in the long traditional slim robes of the 1930s and models moving in mincing steps, much like a damsel in distress, to the current sexy, modern Chinese women walking quickly and confidently. Clothes were changed from the most traditional Chinese *Qi Pao* to the latest modern leather coat trend.

One year later, on 17 April 1998, a road show for Firs named 'Not Me, but the Wind' kicked off in Beijing. The first road show in the history of Chinese fashion, it ran in fifteen Chinese cities, ending on 8 February 1999 in Shanghai at a total cost of 20 million RMB. The road show, broadcast nationwide on local TV stations, was a milestone in the Chinese fashion industry. It was the first time the fashion stage was extended to ordinary people, and, in effect, blew the wind of fashion into the hearts of a multitude of Chinese people. It created many firsts in fashion history with regards to its investment, creativity and scale of the show.

Figure 2.10 The expensive catalogue shot for Firs in Paris
in 1997. Photographer: Wu Hong.

Figure 2.11 The expensive catalogue shot for Firs in Paris in 1997. Photographer: Wu Hong.

Figure 2.12 Catalogue of Firs, 1997.
Photographer: Wang Xin-Yuan.

Though the design duo created many influential fashion events in the industry, they were also embroiled in a controversy. They were given the title of 'show designers', meaning that while they were designers able to present the shows, they were not able to dictate commercial values for the company, given that sales of Firs did not present a prominent achievement. When the contract with Firs expired, the two most famous fashion designers in China left Firs.

A Super 'Impeller' in the Fashion Regime in China

Despite the controversy, Xin-Yuan created many firsts in the regime of fashion in China. He was one of the first sent overseas to study. He was one of the first to launch private labels. Through joint partnership with Zheng Yong-Gang and Zhang Zhao-Da, he raised the income bar of designers in the industry. His achievements in organizing and directing extravagant shows are generally highly praised in the industry; although creating no direct sales revenue, these big events wiped out the once-prevalent grey colour of Chinese clothing and adorned Chinese women's bodies with more colours and sex appeal.

Xin-Yuan's shows were memorable in history in great part due to the innovations he had made in the clothing as well as the format and scale of the shows. His first

Figure 2.13 The 'Night Banquet' show in Tianyi Ge in the city of Ningbo, 1999. Photographer: Pan Jie.

Figure 2.14 The clothes shown at the 'Great Wall Haute
Couture' show, 2000. Photographer: Pan Jie.

Figure 2.15 The show promoting silk fabric in the city of Suzhou, 2001. Photographer: Qian Qi-Er.

mega-scale show—'Into the Sphere of Oriental' (*Zoujin Dongfang*)—was held in the then-largest courtyard in China—the courtyard of Beijing Tian Lun Hotel, a five-star hotel in 1997. The 'Not Me but the Wind' (*Bushi Wo Shi Feng*) tour show directed by him and Zhang Zhao-Da in 1999 made history due to its large expenditure and size of audience reached. The 'Night Banquet' show in the oldest library in China as well as in Asia, Tianyi Ge (built in 1561), interwove the long civil history of China into the fashion language. In 2000 he launched the famous 'Great Wall Haute Couture' show for a local textile miller, Ru Yi Group, and seven years later Karl Lagerfeld had his Fendi show in the same place. In 2001, he directed an innovative skating fashion show for a local down-jacket brand in a skating rink in Beijing. All models were skaters.

From 2000 on, Xin-Yuan has gradually faded into the background of the fashion world. After several trials on building brands, Xin-Yuan finally decided that unless he had an excellent business partner and sufficient funds to invest, he would not start another new brand. He is occasionally seen in the media whenever a profound pundit is needed to speak for the industry: the head of the judge panel for a fashion model contest or designer contest, arts director of another shocking show, critiques

Figure 2.16 The 'Face' collection for a local knitwear brand,
2005. Photographer: Xu Le-Zhong.

Figure 2.17 The 'Face' collection for a local knitwear brand,
2005. Photographer: Xu Le-Zhong.

Figure 2.18 The 'Romance' show for CCTV station, 2006.
Photographer: Wang Jian-Qing.

Figure 2.19 The 'Romance' show for CCTV station, 2006.
Photographer: Wang Jian-Qing.

on any industrial history or issues. He jointly built a company with a friend that pro-vides modelling agency and art director services for fashion events. Now Xin-Yuan spends most of his time in the company, as well as assuming several social roles, such as teaching in the colleges, taking the position of Vice Chairman of the Shanghai

Figure 2.20 The 'China Wind' show for CCTV station, 2007.
Photographer: Wang Jian-Qing.

Figure 2.21 The 'China Wind' show for CCTV station, 2007.
Photographer: Wang Jian-Qing.

Figure 2.22 Sketch by Wang Xin-Yuan. Image courtesy of
Wang Xin-Yuan.

International Fashion Federation, an organization focusing on bridging the gap between Chinese fashion companies and Western fashion partners, and advising clothing entrepreneurs and young designers about designing and branding.

DIALOGUE

In your view, what makes a fashion designer successful?

No matter what you do, I think you need three bricks to achieve your goal, they are: hard work, opportunity and your talents.

From where do you get inspirations for your collection every season?

Life. I think to a sophisticated designer, anything in our daily life can give you inspiration.

In your view, what will drive a Chinese fashion designer into Western mainstream markets?

When our Chinese culture becomes mainstream in the world. And when our GDP per person can compete with those in Europe and the United States.

What do you want people to say about you when one day you retire from the fashion stage?

An impeller of the industry.

WU HAI-YAN: PROFESSOR, DESIGNER AND GENERAL MANAGER

In China, Wu Hai-Yan is a prominent name in clothing as well as in the textile industry. She has been a lecturer and course director of the Textile and Clothing Department, and is now the Vice Dean of the Design Institute of the China Academy of Fine Arts, the oldest Chinese fine arts school. She has been appointed chief designer by large-scale Chinese clothing enterprises. Now she fully owns a design firm providing design and consulting services on clothing, textile, interior design, costume and celebrity styling; she was among the first to start the trend-forecasting system in fashion and textiles for the Chinese market. She was the first champion of the Brother Cup China International Young Fashion Designers Contest, and the recipient of the Golden Fashion Designer Award, the Oscar award of Chinese fashion design. Because of her extensive ability to design with the traditional Chinese fabric

Figure 2.23 Wu Hai-Yan at the 'Vision 2002' show in Beijing, 2001; the model on her right side is the top model Lü Yan. Photographer: Wang Ming-Zhu.

silk, Hai-Yan is always the first name that will be chosen when a clothing designer is needed to create artworks that promote the image of the traditional 'Chinese silk' for the purpose of national culture exchange.

PORTFOLIO

Born: 1958 and now based in the city of Hangzhou, Zhejiang Province.

Education: Graduated with a bachelor's degree in Textile and Clothing Design from Zhejiang Academy of Fine Arts (now China Academy of Fine Arts), 1984.

Career: Professor and course director, Textile and Clothing Department, China Academy of Fine Arts, 1984–present; Chief Designer, Zhejiang Silk Importing & Exporting Co., Hangzhou, 1992–1995; Chief Designer, Hangzhou Kaidi Silk Co. Ltd., Hangzhou, 1995–1997; Chief Designer, China Garment Group, Beijing, 1998–2000; established own design studio, Beijing Wu Hai-Yan Design Firm, 2000–present. Hai-Yan is also the Vice Chairman of the China Fashion Association, Director of

Figure 2.24 Wu Hai-Yan's artwork made in silk. Hand embroidery, hand-painting, spraying, dying and printing are used to accentuate the elegance and beauty of silk. It takes intensive labour to assemble the pieces in order to ensure the prints match perfectly. Photographer: Zhang Da-Peng.

Figure 2.25 Wu Hai-Yan's artwork made in silk.
Photographer: Zhang Da-Peng.

Figure 2.26 Wu Hai-Yan's artwork made in silk.
Photographer: Zhang Da-Peng.

the China Home Textile Committee and member of the National Committee of the Chinese People's Political Consultative Conference.

Selected Awards

1992, first-place prizewinner of the first National Fashion Illustration Contest
1993, first-place prizewinner of the first Brother Cup China International Fashion Designers Contest
1995 and 1997, Top Ten Chinese Fashion Designers Award by CHIC
1999, Golden Award of Design Arts at the National Arts Exhibition, by Ministry of Culture and the National Artists Council
2001, Golden Fashion Designer Award by China Fashion Week

Selected Public Commendations

The majority of Wu Hai-Yan's clothes are made in Chinese silk and linen. She has created an innovative textile prints design by adopting Chinese elements; at the same time her design is trying to achieve a balance between the [Chinese] national spirit and culture and the international trend. (Xinhua Net 2008)

The silk clothing she [Wu Hai-Yan] designed looks elegant and vigorous…Her show once again amazed the spectators: the clothes look elegant and trendy. It is hard for people to believe that silk can be made into such beautiful clothes. She therefore won the top award of China fashion design—the Golden Award. (Bai 1998: 12)

Selected International Exposure

1995, paraded at Dusseldorf Fashion Trade Fair (CPD Dusseldorf), Dusseldorf, Germany
1996, paraded at Tokyo Fashion Week, Tokyo, Japan
1999, paraded at Sino–France Cultural Week, Paris, France
2000, paraded at Sino–U.S Cultural Week, New York, United States
2003, window display in Gallery Lafayette, Paris, France
2004, paraded at the Oriental Impression Sino–France Fashion Week, Paris, France

Selected Publications

'My Views on Clothing Foundation Courses', at the China Clothing and Accessory Forum, 1992

'Pioneering the Reformation of Clothing Education—the Spiral Intertwining of Design Ideas and Technical Capability', at the forum of High Education in Tran-centurial China, 1995

'How Fashion Designers Perceive Fashion Photography', at the academic forum of the Status and Prospect of Fashion Photography in China, 1996

'How Fashion Designers Perceive Textiles', at the forum organized by the China Inter-textile Expo, 1999

'Bridging the Education and Industry through Branding', at the forum organized by Ningbo International Fashion Festival, 2000

The *Quintessential Fashion Design Work of Wu Hai-Yan,* Zhejiang: Zhejiang Science Technology Publishing House, 1994

Fashion Illustration by Wu Hai-Yan, Anhui: Anhui Fine Arts Publishing House, 1997

Brand: WHY

WHY, standing for the first letter of Wu Hai-Yan's name, was registered by her own design firm in 2000. WHY currently offers design service to other companies or individuals instead of being expanded as a private label.

WHY provides design and consulting service in six categories: clothing design, textile design, pattern and graphic design, celebrity styling, trend forecasting and fashion events (exhibition booth design, catwalk show, arts direction, etc.). Her projects included costume design for the wife of the former President of South Korea, Jin Dae-Jung, in 1998, at the request of the State Council; costume design for the finals of the Fifteenth Miss Model of the World held in Istanbul in 2002; clothing design for the country leaders in Asia presented at Bo Ao Asian Forum in the same year.

The design firm now has offices in Beijing and in Wu Hai-Yan's hometown, Hangzhou, with another expected to open in Shanghai in the near future. According to Hai-Yan, the firm makes a meagre profit. When one considers that most of the other Chinese design firms have been short-lived, WHY by contrast has been around for a long time.

BIOGRAPHY

It is difficult to define Wu Hai-Yan with a single word. Her talents cover the spectrum of fashion in design, education and management—three disciplines that normally require different skills. The dichotomy between her outward appearance and demeanor emphasizes her diverse talents: in appearance she is feminine, gentle and sensual; but she proves to be direct, sharp and logical when speaking. She uses both her left and right brain.

A Designer: Tears, Sweat and Dreams (1993–)

Hai-Yan has been fascinated by colours and textures since she was a little girl. When she was a child, she collected candy paper in all kinds of fancy colours, and salvaged fabrics that were used by her grandmother for making bed sheets. Sketching on papers or books was another childhood hobby. Hai-Yan never received any professional instruction in painting, but her artistic flair carried over into adulthood, when she registered for a design course without hesitation.

After winning the first Brother Cup China International Young Fashion Designers Contest in 1993 (she won the only Golden Award), Hai-Yan came to the public's attention. Her work, named 'The Generation of Prosperity', was inspired by her visit to the Mogao Grottoes[3] ten years before. She was amazed by the magnificent carved

Figure 2.27 'The Generation of Prosperity' helped Wu Hai-Yan win the first-place prize in 1993. Photographer: Jin Huang.

Buddha stones and the gorgeous paintings left by the Chinese ancestors, and ten years later the memory of those images inspired her entry in the design contest. With the soulful music of Enya playing, the painting-like clothes transmitted the emotion between ancient China and cosmopolitan China. It convinced the hearts of spectators as well as the sharp eyes of the judges' panel composed of international experts and local professors.

The awards also brought Hai-Yan to the attention of the fashion industry. In the early 1990s, when many private companies were emerging, a businessman approached her about a partnership to start a new fashion brand. While Hai-Yan was excited about the opportunity to devote herself to brand building, she discovered that the partner used her fame to get a loan from the bank. The worst part of their relationship was their different philosophies in brand building. The partner, without consulting Hai-Yan, built a production factory with the majority of the funding, while Hai-Yan expected the borrowed money to be invested in building distribution channels. China has more than 10,000 garment factories and Hai-Yan felt they could outsource the production. It was no surprise that the venture eventually failed.

She was then invited to join a large enterprise called Kaidi Silk Company in Hangzhou. Hai-Yan worked for Kaidi for two years before an incident caused her to leave the company.

One day when she was working in the office, a group of Japanese men together with an interpreter visited her. She was surprised to learn they were from the giant Japanese group, Mitsubishi, and that she had been under observation for half a year. They had read any articles they could find about her, and visited all of her shows. They felt Hai-Yan had great potential to succeed world-wide and they wanted to promote her to an international level. The conversation even included plans for the first show to be an extravagant fall-winter collection in the famous Summer Palace in Beijing. Remembering the experience years later, Hai-Yan was still impressed by the wealthy stance of the tycoons. She was told that Mitsubishi could invest billions in promoting her, and they believed no enterprise in China would be as talented and daring.

This dialogue took place when Hai-Yan was preparing for her parade for the first China Fashion Week in 1997. They reached an agreement that Mitsubishi would be the financial sponsor for her parade, and they would sign an official contract right after the show. However, the company presented Hai-Yan with a big stack of paper—the contract—before the opening of the show and asked her to sign. Hai-Yan consulted a lawyer friend and understood that once she signed the contract, all the intellectual property of her design work, her parades, even her portrait, would be owned by Mitsubishi instead of by herself; all her speeches and public activities would also need pre-approval from Mitsubishi. The contract was for fifteen years. Hai-Yan didn't know how to play by the international game rules. Fear over losing her freedom, and uncertainty about future prospects, finally led her to abandon the opportunity. She was asked to return all the money Mitsubishi had spent to fund her collections. Borrowing money from an entrepreneur friend, she was able to pay off the debt.

However, trouble always seems to come in pairs. At the fashion week, Hai-Yan was defeated by her rival Zhang Zhao-Da, in competition for the Golden Fashion Designer Award of the year. The competition had been the hottest topic in the fashion media because it was the first Golden Fashion Designer Award reception, and both competitors were the most prominent in the country. Tears gushed from her eyes when she heard the final result on the stage. Many spectators of her show had told her she would definitely win, and she was ranked at the top by both the media judge panel and the academic judge panel. But she was listed below Zhang Zhao-Da by the entrepreneur panel. Shanshan sponsored Zhang Zhao-Da at the time, and the company was also a member of the entrepreneur judge panel—Hai-Yan lost her sponsor as well as the first-place award.

Life is sometimes a comedy of errors and you never know what is going to happen next. The day after the award ceremony, Hai-Yan was asked to stay in Beijing to be the chief designer for a new company financed by the China Garment Group. The China Garment Group, one of the largest state-owned clothing enterprises, was under the direct administration of the Ministry of Textiles at the time. Hai-Yan was promised shares and attractive prospects. Persuaded, Hai-Yan joined the new company. But the disordered economic infrastructure at the time once again gave Hai-Yan a severe attack of nerves. Not long after she joined the company, she found out that somehow someone in the company forged her signature illegally and sold her shares to others—she was cheated again and had to leave her position.

The typical Chinese philosophy of 'having a friend is better than having an enemy' finally convinced her to not take legal action against the company. Once again she was at a crossroads in her life: go back to Hangzhou or stay in Beijing and find another job? She had just bought a new house in Beijing, and now she could not even afford to pay the mortgage. If she went back to Hangzhou, she would be in disgrace because all her friends in her hometown knew she was a big designer for a large company. Hai-Yan walked the streets for a few days, trying to decide what to do. During this time, she was presented with many attractive opportunities, all of which proved to be false. Someone even told her he could help her open a shop on Fifth Avenue in Manhattan. In the end, she found that life is the best educator, and it taught Hai-Yan that she should start her own business. Thus began the WHY brand.

With no investor funds, she had to use her own small savings. That was in the year 2000. Fortunately, a design studio is easier to start up than other ventures and costs relatively little to run. Hai-Yan is quite happy with the performance of the firm, though it only makes a meagre profit. It's a miracle to her that she has been able to carry on the business for eight years (by the time of this interview) while many design studios in China were short-lived due to the harsh economic environment. Now WHY is one of the best-known design studios in China, and Hai-Yan believes her painstaking work will eventually help her realize her goal.

A Professor at the China Academy of Fine Arts: An Academic Designer and Pragmatic Professor (1984–)

Hai-Yan has achieved as much in fashion education as she has in the design industry. Her nearly twenty years of experience provided the 'campus' for her education.

There has long been a controversy over whether college instructors should have jobs outside the campus. For applied sciences or arts (such as fashion education), some people agree the lecturer should obtain practical experience in the industry, while others argue that it dilutes the lecturers' focus. Hai-Yan has been criticized for commuting between campus and business, but she has proved that the two complement each other.

The China Academy of Fine Arts was built in 1928 and has been one of the top arts schools in China. It recruits only 1,500 students out of more than 80,000 applicants each year.

After being promoted to Course Director of the Textile and Clothing Department, the first thing Hai-Yan did was to reform the course structure and syllabus. Her goal was to ensure that all the programs were pragmatic rather than academic, while maintaining the traditional Chinese craftsmanship that has been the quintessential specialty of the institute since it was built.

The four-year bachelor program in the China Academy of Fine Arts is now more systematic. The first year covers foundation courses in graphic design and three-dimensional design, pencil sketching and watercolour painting, expanding in the second year to programs focusing on traditional Chinese arts, including Chinese line drawing, meticulous drawing, embroidery techniques and hand textile painting. Hai-Yan believes that learning the ancient skills of the ancestors not only widens the spectrum of design but is also a strategy to emphasize the difference between Chinese designers and Western designers. In the third year the concentration switches to clothing design and technology, including designing, cutting and sewing. At the same time, students are asked to learn market research, photography and fashion styling. The final year is all about project workshops and best practice. There is no doubt that working in the industry ties Hai-Yan strongly to local enterprises, and these become the workshop base for her students.

The reform took about five years before Hai-Yan was satisfied. Most of the resistance came from the older faculty. To achieve her goal she had to first upgrade the knowledge of old ones and recruit young ones who had both industrial and academic experience. The most difficult part was to upgrade the overall quality of the older teachers. In the academic institutions of China, older teachers historically had permanent contracts. Their age and experience became a double-edged sword when faced with reform. Hai-Yan had offended some of the older faculty during her reform work. Because the older ones 'had been teaching when Wu was still a young girl', they refused to change the syllabus and teaching mode, believing their way was better.

Compared to most other professors, Hai-Yan's frequent exposure to the international market and experience gained from her firm helped her truly understand what types of designers were needed in the industry, hence what subjects should be covered in school and what methodology should be adopted for the classes. With 12 full-time teachers in her department and approximately 300 students, with 20 students in each class, she felt proud of every achievement her students made. One student received first place in the national design contest. Another was admitted to the first-class design school, Central Saint Martin School of Design and Arts. Businesses asked for more graduates.

DIALOGUE

You were the first person who started the trend-forecasting system in China. Can you elaborate on what it is and how it works?

I started to do trend forecasting in 1994. Every year I publicize the forecasting results via shows and printed books. Before, I did it with the China Colour Trend Association, but now I do it under the name of my design studio. It was a panic at the beginning. We had no funding, neither had we experience. But I knew it was the right thing to do. The hard part was that few people understood why the industry needed trend forecasting or what it was for. These printed books included all the research we had done, and we gave them away free to companies. The good news is that now most people understand the need and they come to my company to buy the forecasting brochures.

Trend forecasting is all about research and analysis. In general our research included the international designers' shows, street snapshots of people, window displays, professional magazines and international fashion fairs. We study fiber, fabric, pattern, graphics, colour and design. Any new artistic or cultural tide is another important resource for us, such as music, painting, visual arts, or even philosophical ideology. Once we collect all the information, we group all the data and analyse their

Figure 2.28 Wu Hai-Yan's early work, 1989.
Photographer: Huang Zheng-Xiong.

Figure 2.29 The collection *Qi Cheng Zhuan He* won the
Golden Award of Design Arts at the National Arts Exhibition
in 1999. Photographer: Pan Jie.

Figure 2.30 The collection *Qi Cheng Zhuan He*.
Photographer: Pan Jie.

Figure 2.31 The collection *Qi Cheng Zhuan He.*
Photographer: Pan Jie.

Figure 2.32 The collection *Qi Cheng Zhuan He*.
Photographer: Pan Jie.

Figure 2.33 The 'Oriental Silk' show near the West Lake in
the city of Hangzhou, 2001. Photographer: Ge Hai-Feng.

Figure 2.34 The 'Oriental Silk' show near the West Lake in the city of Hangzhou, 2001. Photographer: Ge Hai-Feng.

isomorphism. Fashion has a lifecycle, regardless of its short or long life, and all fashion experiences a period of introduction, growth, maturity and decline. We use lifecycle theory and our analytical results to predict the trends of the next one to two years.

In general trend forecasting is a complicated process, and we need more companies and people to participate. It is not something that can be achieved by any individual or a company.

Chinese designers have been criticized for copying many of the Western brands. Now the government is advocating 'original design'. Do you think we have original-designed brands?

To answer your question, we first have to understand what original design is. [Drawing a cup on a piece of paper.] Here is a cup that someone has invented a long time ago. Now you want to design a new cup. You can

Figure 2.35 The 'Vision 2002' show in the famous 798 Artistic
Centre in Beijing, 2001. Photographer: Wang Ming-Zhu.

easily just change the colour and the material but keep it the same shape.
Is this original design or plagiarism? You know it is very common in the
design regime to hear someone say he got inspiration from someone's
work. It is not plagiarism.

Figure 2.36 The 'Vision 2002' show in the famous 798 Artistic
Centre in Beijing, 2001. Photographer: Wang Ming-Zhu.

Figure 2.37 The 'Oriental Impression' show at Sino–France
Fashion Week in Paris, 2004. Photographer: Wang Wei.

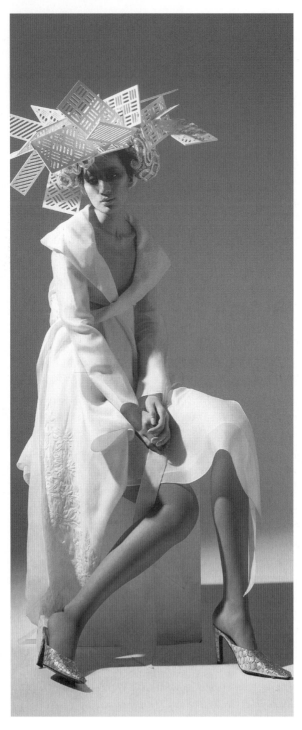

Figure 2.38 The 'Echo of Oriental Silk' show, 2006.
Photographer: Zhang Da-Peng.

I once met a lawyer who was working on the intellectual property issue. With regards to clothing design, he was unsure what the boundary was between plagiarism and original design. I recommended that he adopt the musical staff to assess the issue. [Drawing the musical staff.] The musical staff normally has five lines, though of course we could create as many lines as we needed. Each line represents a component of clothing design: shape, fabric, colour, pattern, graphic and structure…Now, mark points to symbolize where each design corresponds closest to each component. The more similarity the two designs have, the closer the two points are. Join all the points and eventually you should get two curved lines. Now you should see how close the two are, and how many components are at the same point or at a nearby point. I think it is a good way to differentiate between plagiarism and original design. So once we have a clear definition on the 'original design' I think it is easier to develop an authentic original design.

You've been working in the college for more than twenty years, and you've visited many international schools. What are the major differences between the Chinese education system and the Western education system?

To be honest I'm quite proud of our education system. When we receive visitors from other colleges or overseas schools, they always tell me how impressed they are, and they would like to learn from us. When I visited some of the fashion schools in Germany and France, I noticed in Europe the programs were divided into segments. For instance, textile prints only teaches textile—they don't teach you anything about clothing. Clothing design mostly focuses on design, and they don't teach you much about fabric science or marketing. Cutting only teaches you cutting, and all you can do is be a cutter after you graduate. The problem with such a system is that graduates have niche jobs, option for jobs. Because the design students cannot cut, neither can they work in textile companies. In addition, hand-embroidery and other types of traditional craftsmanship will be extinct because it is hard to find a job if you only have the traditional craftsmanship skills. The only way for these old techniques to survive is to integrate them into new programs. I think in college the students should have their focused subjects but at the same time learn the related subjects. Our clothing design students also spend time learning fabric science and marketing, so when they graduate, they may become a pattern designer for a textile firm or a buyer for a fashion company. In general we provide more integrated and comprehensive programs for our students.

What made you become a fashion designer?

I loved painting ever since I was a little kid. Even today when I meet my childhood friends, they always mention how much I liked painting. In fact I failed the first time when I took the entry exam at the China Academy of Fine Arts in 1978. In 1980 I tried the second time and succeeded.

Where do you get inspirations for your collection every season?

You know many people talk about 'inspiration'. They see something in life that inspires them just like an ignited spark. I think to a sophisticated designer life's experiences are like a big reservoir for design inspiration. The more I experience, the more I understand about life, and the better I can translate my understanding about life to my design. Of course I also monitor trends. You know, I started the trend-forecasting system more than ten years ago. The global artistic or cultural influence or trend is another big issue I pay attention to. For instance, music, films, fine arts, or even any new philosophical ideology.

What do you think makes you such a successful designer?

Am I successful? No, I don't think so yet. I still have a long way to go. I want to be like Armani [Laughs.]... I think I'm just a persistent person in pursuit of my dream. And the two things that have supported such persistence are my passion and commitment to design.

What is your ultimate goal?

Like many other designers, my dream is to see my private label in the international market. Now I am on my way. Ten years ago, my first goal was to be a famous designer in China, and I made it; then I told myself I should start my own design firm and it must be profitable, now I made that true as well; my next target is to build my own label, instead of only providing design service to others. I know it is tough, but I am patient. Armani did not start his first shop until he was nearly forty, and he did not become famous until he was over fifty. Now he is over seventy but still working. So I think step-by-step, as long as each step is solid enough, I will make it.

In your view, what will drive a Chinese fashion designer into Western mainstream markets?

Let me give you an example first. In 1999 I went to Paris to see the Kenzo show. After the show I got to know the art director of the show through a friend. And I asked him if I went to Paris for a parade if he would like to be my art director. He said of course but I must be prepared to spend money—4 million in Ren Min Bi at least (at the time), including all the media promotion and the parade itself.

So you know what I mean—money. Whenever we can get strong financial support. In other words, when the economic power in China becomes large enough to support Chinese designers to go to the Western market, I think we will make the dream become true. Of course culture is another important factor—when Chinese culture integrates into the mainstream global culture, it will also help Chinese designers. I don't think Chinese fashion designers are weak in design compared to the Western designers. On the contrary I think we have excellent designers now in the local market. We just need to be patient and wait for the overall environment to become more favorable to the growth of Chinese designers.

How do you recruit a designer?

Before, I recruited designers based on their qualifications in school. I normally only hired the top five students. I did like to recruit fresh graduates so they could be trained my way. But later I found it was a mistake. I once hired a design student who had just obtained a master's degree. She received distinction when she studied in college. She showed her graphic design works to me, and all the works looked excellent to me. So I hired her. One month later, when I was reading an arts magazine, my eyes were caught by the graphics in the book. They looked so familiar to me—they were exactly the same as the works presented by the student. I was very surprised. Obviously she lied to me. Back at the office, I asked her again if the work she had shown me was her own. She said it was. When I showed her the magazine, she cried and asked for my forgiveness. I fired her because I hate to be lied to. It taught me a lesson: no matter how good the candidate is in design skills, ethics are more important than anything else.

When was the first time you went abroad? Where was it? And how did you feel about the trip?

My first trip overseas was when I went to Hong Kong in 1993. It was a reward for winning the Brother Cup. Before I went to Hong Kong,

I carefully chose the best outfit in my wardrobe. It was a grey sweater mixed with a pale beige skirt. While it may not have looked trendy to Hong Kong people, I thought at least it was not something out of mode. When I arrived in Hong Kong, I felt so ashamed. No one wore sweaters in Hong Kong, and my style signified I was from the mainland. [Laughing] The trip showed me how backwards we were compared to an international city.

My trip to Paris in 1995 was also very impressive. I went to Paris with Wang Xin-Yuan and Liu Yang. It was the first time any of us had been to Paris. I still remember when we arrived at the airport and took the coach to the downtown hotel, we sat in the bus and all remained quiet. A few minutes later, Liu Yang gazed at the blue sky and whispered, 'How come the moon in the West is brighter than it is in China?' [Laughing] Then I said, 'Well, they have cleaner air.' Xin-Yuan followed, saying, 'Their street is cleaner.' [Laughing again] You know it was just such a different world to all of us ten years ago...

Do you have any Western designers that you admire?

I don't have a specific idol I admire, but I respect every designer. I think every designer has his or her glitter. I like the elegance of Yves Saint Laurent as well as the straight cutting of Pierre Cardin. I was fascinated by the courage of Jean Paul Gautier, and John Galliano always amazes the world with his theatrical shows.

What was your experience when you visited the design houses in Europe the first time?

Pierre Cardin impressed me a lot. He was also the first Western designer I became acquainted with. I still remember when I visited his studio the first time, I noticed a stack of pictures on his bookshelf. They were all very beautiful photographs of architecture. One of the photos showed a pair of 'eyes' on the mountain. In the darkness of the picture the eyes were very impressive, and I discovered they were actually an architecture created to look like eyes from a distance. I had seen this photo before when I was in school, so when I saw it again I recognized it. Mr. Cardin told me that the architecture was his design. It was such a surprise to me because I never expected a clothing designer could also be an architectural designer. But after so many years of a career in design, now I truly believe there are common languages in arts design.

FRANKIE XIE: A HETEROGENEOUS DESIGNER

Frankie Xie is one of the few Chinese designers who obtained his education degree and work experience in the two most influential fashion capitals: Tokyo and Paris in the 1980s and 1990s. He started his own brand, Jefen, in 2000, and is one of the most commercially successful designers now in China. Frankie is also the first Chinese designer that successfully launched his international debut at the top four international fashion weeks—Paris, London, Milan and New York. Search 'Jefen by Frankie' on Yahoo, and 35,100 results will be displayed. To date, this is the largest number of hits on a Chinese fashion designer that could be found on an English Web site.

PORTFOLIO

Born: in the city of Hangzhou, Zhejiang Province, 1960. Now based in Beijing.

Education: Graduated with a bachelor's degree in Textile Design from Zhejiang Institute of Silk Science, 1984; graduated with a master's degree in Fashion Design from Bunka College of Fashion, Tokyo, 1990.

Figure 2.39 Frankie Xie and his models at Paris Fashion Week. Photographer: Pan Jie.

· **Career:** Fashion Design lecturer, Zhejiang Institute of Silk Science, 1984–1988; designer for a line of Madame Nicole, Matsuda Nicole Ltd., Tokyo, 1990–1993; designer, Kenzo's company, Paris, 1993–1995; Design Director, Matsuda Nicole Ltd., Hong Kong office, 1996–1998; Chief Designer, San.San Li brand, Beijing, 1998–1999; formed own brand Jefen, 2000.

Selected Public Commendations

Last year, on October 1, Xie took his six-year-old label Jefen to Paris and kicked off the eight-day Paris Fashion Week with the youthful spring/summer collection 'The Door' at the Louvre. It marked the first time a Chinese fashion house was taking part in the event. Didier Grumbach, president of the French Couture Federation, says that he believes Xie's appearance on the official calendar of the Paris Fashion Week will have 'an enormous impact in China'. (Chen 2007)

The L'Agence France-Presse, the Associated Press and Reuters all released a piece of news with images of the show from its first minute. The Web site of the *British Daily Telegraph* published ten photos from the show; the fashion Web site FlipZone posted forty-four large images. The famous 'the most serious newspaper' *Le Monde* mentioned the name of China brand Jefen at the opening of Paris Fashion Week: 'Paris, as the capital of design, revealed the design and style from the Orient, [in the brand] Jefen, from China…' the commentators mentioned and affirmed his mixed-and-balanced design style coming forth from the show…(Yan 2008: 189)

Xie Feng is continuing the dream of China fashion in Paris. This season Jefen, with the theme, 'Harmony', revealed a spirit of balance: balance between consumer trends and living pressures, balance between different cultures…The Chinese dragon scale, the layered embroidery, the voluminous fur and comfortable down jacket are displayed in a format of European style. Xie Feng is demonstrating a subtle luxuriousness with a soft tone by balancing between elegant rhythm and strong seduction. (Li and Jin 2008: 104)

Two years ago, the whole world remembered the name of Xie Feng—the first Chinese designer who was invited to present at the Paris Fashion Week and who amazed the spectators at the top-class fashion week by his gorgeous Chinese collection. Two years later, after the four consecutive parades at the Paris Pret-a-Porter shows in the Louvre, Xie Feng carried his Jefen line confidently into the on-schedule shows of the Paris Fashion Week. Some of the local fashion syllabus even included his case into the study of Fashion History. (*Harper's Bazaar China* 2008: 13)

Selected Publication

Fashion Journey (*Shishang zhilu*), China Textile Publishing House, 2004

Brand: Jefen

Jefen, founded by Frankie Xie and his wife in 2000, targets sophisticated elite busi-nesswomen, ages thirty to forty-five, who are well educated, earn high incomes and know their wardrobes well. Its price ranges from 1,000–5,000 RMB. Jefen has the Italian romantic and feminine touch, blended with the oriental pragmatic and hum-ble. Jefen now has approximately thirty shops, most directly operated, in large cities like Beijing and Shanghai. Its turnover is more than 100 million RMB (by the time of this interview).

BIOGRAPHY

Frankie's great-grandfather, Xie Da-Ao, was one of the One Hundred Children[4] who were dispatched to the United States for overseas study by the Qing government in the mid-nineteenth century. He married an occidental woman while he lived in the States, who later gave birth to Frankie's grandfather. This explains why Frankie's sculptured face is different from typical flat Chinese faces.

His blended lineage of occidental and oriental, plus his long journey from Tokyo to Paris to Milan to Hong Kong and then to Beijing left a diverse imprint on him. He has the precision of the Japanese, the romance of the Parisians, the sophistication of the Milanese and—the most radical—the philosophical ideology of the Chinese.

Fashion Design Course Founder (1980–1988)

Because he graduated with a degree in textile design in 1984 from the Zhejiang In-stitute of Silk Science, Frankie was asked to stay at the school to start up the fashion design course. At the time, Frankie was twenty-four and had very little knowledge of fashion design, and the isolation of China in the mid 1980s meant limited sources for the teaching curriculum. All the teachers had to find textbooks and other documents for teaching on their own, then had to learn the books through self-study.

The Sino–Japanese relations in the beginning of the 1980s made Japanese a popu-lar foreign language in Chinese colleges. The Japanese curriculum of fashion courses consequently became a vital resource and reference for young lecturers like Frankie Xie. Every night, Frankie translated the Japanese textbooks into Chinese and then taught what he translated to his students the next day.

The more challenging task was to find projects for the students. Frankie knew that the students would not be able to learn the essentials of the course without practicing what they learned. In the early 1980s, when there were no Chinese fashion brands yet, few garment factories had need of designers. In Hangzhou, where the school is located, the only factory that could provide design projects for students was the

Zhejiang Silk Importing & Exporting Group, which was the largest textile importing and exporting company in the province. Of course, they needed clothing designs in order to attract overseas traders to buy their fabrics. But their needs were very limited because all they required were a few pieces of sample clothing using their fabrics. To make matters worse, Frankie's college often had to compete with another fashion institute in the same city—Zhejiang Academy of Fine Arts (now China Academy of Fine Arts)—for the only available projects.

The most difficult hurdle presented itself when the first group of students graduated. They found themselves jobless because in the 1980s all garment manufacturers had to do was copy patterns from overseas suppliers, then put them into production. Hence, no one needed a designer. To find jobs for the students, Frankie traveled to the city of Shenzhen with them, a city that had the most foreign-invested garment factories at the time due to its proximity to Hong Kong and an open-door policy to foreign investors. In Shenzhen, they visited several garment factories that were jointly invested and managed by Chinese and Westerners. Frankie still remembers when they visited a factory that manufactured underwear for overseas buyers. The students were amazed at the sexy bras made with intricate and elegant lace. Until then, all bras sold in the Chinese market were one colour and one style and were made of plain cotton fabric with no padding inside.

Four years of teaching and a lack of design information finally forced Frankie to decide to go to Japan to study. With an ambitious dream to be a great fashion designer like Yves Saint Laurent—one of the few designer names known by the Chinese at the time—he believed he needed further education to attain his goal.

Bunka College of Fashion (1989–1990)

With the loan of 10,000 RMB from friends, Frankie arrived in Tokyo in 1989, and a modern building in central downtown came into view—the Bunka College of Fashion.

The first class at Bunka gave fresh insight to Frankie. In China, fashion design was very much like a drawing course; illustration was a key part of the curriculum. The majority of the time during a one-week course would be spent on fashion drawing. However, in the first class at Bunka, all the students were asked to wrap a stone with a piece of fabric without creating wrinkles or creases in the fabric. The only tools the students had were a stone, a piece of fabric and scissors.

Frankie noticed the essential difference between the two education systems: Chinese education taught flat drawing, so all students had excellent drawing skills, but the designs were based on two dimensions. The Japanese method had used a three-dimensional system from the beginning, since the human body is three-dimensional.

'Modelling' was the first idea introduced into Frankie's head at Bunka, and this concept eventually allowed him to be an excellent draper in his fashion design career.

Lifestyle was the second lesson Frankie learned from Bunka. Not long after the class concluded, the professor asked all students to participate in an experimental lifestyles program. The program was conducted in a five-star hotel in Tokyo, and all students would eat dinner there wearing formal dress. To a student from China, whose monthly income was only 70 RMB at the time and who had taken out a loan of 10,000 RMB, going to a five-star hotel was an intimidating experience. Though he wore the best suit he'd ever owned, Frankie was still embarrassed when he found himself in extreme contrast to the luxurious environment of the hotel; even the waiters wore higher-quality suits than his. The late dinner program was the most nervous dinner in his life: it was French cuisine, and he had to learn to use twenty-four different types of forks and spoons in the process of enjoying the food.

The lifestyle program taught Frankie that a designer needs to understand the lifestyle of the high-class people who are the primary consumers of designer brand products. At the same time Frankie learned that designs didn't simply appear out of thin air; they were rooted in life experience. Therefore, to be a first-class designer he needed to understand high-class social life, and also that there are no good clothes or bad clothes, just the 'right clothes' for the right time and the right occasion.

To afford the expensive tuition and living expenses in Tokyo, Frankie had to take a part-time job after school. Washing dishes in restaurants was the most common job held by Chinese students in Japan, but the pay was very low. Hampered by unreasonable rules, Frankie was once paid for only one day when he actually had worked seven days of that week, all because he was late to work.

His life took a dramatic turn after an accident at the nearby train station. Frankie was hit by a motorcyclist while he was riding his bicycle. Spectators thought he was near death, but the doctor who examined him told him he had nothing more than a light scratch and no other problems. Frankie remembered the Chinese saying 'Skipping from a big disaster means a great fortune', and indeed good fortune came to pass.

To gain more experience, Frankie attended the Second Nippon Young Designers Fashion Contest in 1990. The theme of the contest was to design clothes for cleaning women. The clothes needed to be utilitarian, aesthetic and fashionable. Inspired by Japanese architecture, Frankie created a dress that was simple, modern and geometrical in its look. The illustration immediately received qualification to move into the next phase of the contest. Then he spent one month making the clothing while he awaited the results of the contest.

After two months of anxious waiting, the awards party was held in a famous theatre in Tokyo, one of the most luxurious locations in the city. Not knowing who would be the final winner, Frankie dressed in a formal suit. The awards ranged from Excellence to Bronze to Silver, with the prestigious Golden Award being the highly coveted top award. Frankie was hoping for Excellence, until the Silver winner was announced and he thought he would not be receiving any award at all. Then the MC announced the winner: Frankie Xie, for the Golden Award. Tears filled Frankie's eyes; for a young student from China who still had to work part-time while studying to support himself and who was considered a grass-roots designer, the award was a dream come true.

Frankie immediately went from a lower-class lifestyle to middle-class. He became famous in school, and NHK TV station and other local media reported the talents of the young Chinese designer. The Golden Award brought 250,000 Japanese yen income for Frankie every month, an 80,000 Japanese yen bonus, and a 170,000 Japanese yen payment from the Matsuda Nicole company, which subsequently employed Frankie as a part-time designer after the awards show. Given that in the 1980s a manager's income was 170,000 Japanese yen, Frankie became the richest student in the school and was able to quit his part-time dishwashing job.

Nicole Ltd. Tokyo and Kenzo in Paris (1990–1995)

Right after his graduation, Frankie was employed full-time by Nicole. Nicole was founded in the 1960s by designer Mitsuhiro Matsuda, a close friend of Kenzo. Nicole was one of the famous brands in Japan in the 1980s and 1990s, owning more than 500 shops all over the world, including the international markets of the United States and England. The design firm was the equivalent of Issey Miyake, Junya Watanabei and Kenzo in Japan.

Frankie worked for Madame Nicole as an assistant designer. Two years after he was hired he was promoted to assistant to Mitsuhiro Matsuda himself because of his excellent performance.

A November 1989 article in *Women's Wear Daily* commented, 'Few can tread the fine line between sophistication and adventure the way Mitsuhiro Matsuda does.' Matsuda defined a kind of practical aesthetic dress of the late-twentieth century, and continued to make unique fashion inroads in the early 2000s. Matsuda liked using Western tailoring mixed with oriental details, which influenced Frankie's designs later (fashionencyclopedia.com).

There are seven brands under Nicole, making the company a key player for Tokyo Fashion Week and New York Fashion Week. For Frankie, and all other designers in the company, preparing for the fashion shows was a major part of their work.

Because of the close relationship between Matsuda and Kenzo, Frankie had a chance to work for Kenzo in 1994–1995 in Paris. Because Kenzo was not involved in sales and marketing himself, his office was more like a design studio which employed designers from different countries. Most of Kenzo's inspiration came from his travels, and he liked to pass the source of his inspiration on to other designers so they could use it in their designs. Frankie was very impressed when Kenzo traveled to Africa and took pictures of colourful African flowers. When he returned, he showed a picture of a floral scene, covered by a see-through paper. When someone tried to remove the paper to more clearly see the picture, Kenzo prevented him and told him to look through the piece of paper, 'You will see a different picture and that is how you should develop your design.'

Frankie's work experience at Nicole, and Kenzo's guidance, allowed him to understand the essence of design—that is, to find beauty from life. He began to understand that a person whose own quality of life was lacking would not be a good designer.

Back to China (1998–2000)

In 1998, ten years after he'd left China, Frankie settled in Beijing because he was sure Beijing was the only city in China that could afford a designer. The city is located in north China and has an altitude of 45 degrees, which is the same altitude as Paris, New York and Tokyo.

Offered 1 million RMB in remuneration, Frankie signed a contract with San Li Group, the group that produced yarn. The group planned to launch 'San.San Li', a brand targeting businesswomen who wanted casual office wear.

Frankie's excitement at returning to his hometown was soon replaced with the reality of life in China at the time. He launched a successful show for the brand, but soon found his customers could not purchase the products, although they said they liked the clothes very much. The first issue he encountered was sizing; all the clothes were made based on the standard size of Chinese women, but the stagnancy in sales indicated that the clothes could not be worn by Chinese women. When he asked his customers, he began to understand that in winter time northern Chinese women always liked to wear a sweater underneath a jacket to keep warm. Westerners, on the other hand, preferred to wear only a shirt or a jersey top underneath a jacket. Then he found the one-button jacket with a lapel collar did not sell as well as he thought because the low neckline revealed the underwear beneath. Normally customers want a jacket to have two or three buttons so their underwear won't be seen, especially since their underwear may be old.

More trouble was ahead. Frankie recruited three assistants from Japan and a merchandising manager from Hong Kong, all poised for the start of the reform in the country. But he soon found he could not get support from his financial partners. His lack of understanding of the local markets was driving down sales. The working philosophy of the local people and the lack of standards, processes and systems had Frankie working in an isolated environment. Like most of the other chief designers who were making millions, he finally had to leave the company after two years.

Birth of Jefen: From Surrealism to Realism (2000–)

In 2000, after his fashion show at China Fashion Week, an American approached Frankie and expressed interest in looking for a Chinese designer to expand his company's fashion business in China. The company was an Italian textile miller—Jiegna.

Jiegna, one of the oldest textile firms in Italy, was founded in the nineteenth century. The current owner, Mr. William, was a kind, generous, supportive, tasteful, old man in Frankie's eyes. At one time, William supported Giorgio Armani when Armani was young and expanding his own business. William permitted Armani to buy fabric from him on credit and pay him back after he sold the clothes. This time, William gave the same support to Frankie; he believed in Frankie's potential in China.

In 2000, with a 300,000 RMB investment and fabric supplied by Jiegna, Frankie and his wife opened a small boutique in Beijing. His wife graduated from the Central Theatrical Institute, the same school as Zhang Zi-Yi, the Chinese movie star most famous outside of China. The unique designs at the boutique received attention from the local high-end department stores and Jefen soon became a high-end local designer brand in Beijing.

Jefen targeted women aged thirty to forty-five, well-educated, with high incomes and good taste—modern, sophisticated Chinese women. In 2001, half of the women in an EMBA (Executive Master of Business Administration) class at Beijing University were wearing Jefen at prices between 1,000 and 4,000 RMB.

Jefen's casual office wear mixed romance and independence. It was made for a woman, but not overly feminine. A signature ensemble was a suit jacket and skirt in silver grey with intricate embroidery and design details.

Targeting the couture customer, Frankie was not overly anxious to expand the business. He was more interested in staying true to his core customer and his quality craftsmanship.

The goal of every designer is to be treated with respect from the department stores. Anyone doing business with department stores in China knows of their dictatorial ways. As the mainstay of Chinese retail, department stores are very arrogant. To get into the stores, brands not only need financial backing, but also close relationships with the stores' managers themselves. Brands that are small or young are often moved from one counter to another or even kicked out of the store altogether before the expiration of their contracts, if sales are poor. Jefen has been well respected because

Figure 2.40 Jefen's line. Photographer: Pan Jie.

it is able to sell more than 10 million RMB per year in a high-end department store such as the Saite store in Beijing.

Six years after the founding of the brand, Jefen was becoming a more welcomed local designer brand in China. Its high-end shops in Beijing and Shanghai and its 1,000-square-meter office in central Beijing are symbols of its financial growth. When interviewed, Frankie said he and his wife had earned enough money in the six years to live comfortably for the rest of their lives. Their next objective was to provide that same financial security to their employees and later to spread the wealth to society in general.

Jefen was one of the few successes among the first generation of Chinese designers. Frankie was low key in his media exposure and practical in his designs. Balancing art and commerce, he wanted his designs to be unique, but at the same time wearable by his target consumers. With his wife managing the business, he could focus on design.

Entry to Paris Fashion Week (2006–)

Supported and financed by a French luxury consulting company after a strict evaluation process, Jefen was invited to the 2007 Spring/Summer Paris Fashion Week. The international debut was paraded on 1 October 2006, the Chinese National Holiday. As a way of welcoming the Chinese design guru, it was arranged for Jefen to be the first one of all the shows. Frankie used 'door' as the name of the show, to symbolize that the door of Chinese fashion brands is open to the international mainstream market. It was the first show presented by a Chinese fashion designer in one of the most

Figure 2.41 Jefen's image. Photographer: Pan Jie.

Figure 2.42 Jefen 2009 Spring/Summer image.
Photographer: Li Zi.

influential international fashion weeks, and it was truly a commercial show rather than an exhibition or entertainment show.

The show in Paris also proved to be a great contribution to the sales growth in its China market. Unlike most other local designers who only enjoyed fame but produced no revenue from the market share, Frankie saw Jefen gradually became a typical symbol of Chinese designer brands.

DIALOGUE

What do you see as the prospect for Chinese fashion designer brands?

The era of fashion design is over. Now everything is dominated by rich companies like LVMH, Gucci. I feel quite pessimistic about the future of designers. I think eventually designers' work will be controlled and guided by those giant fashion firms. I don't think designers will have a chance anymore to start from scratch and build a giant brand, like Armani did, or any other successful designer brands have done in the past. Because the giants will force you to merge with them. If you have potential, they

Figure 2.43 Jefen 2009 Spring/Summer image.
Photographer: Li Zi.

Figure 2.44 Jefen 2009 Spring/Summer image.
Photographer: Li Zi.

Figure 2.45 Jefen 2009 Spring/Summer image.
Photographer: Li Zi.

either buy you out, or make you die if you refuse to sell. The market is very crucial, I've seen so many formerly successful designers go bankrupt or be kicked out of the brand office.

As a designer who has been studying and working overseas, what do you think of Chinese fashion designers?

I watch few Chinese fashion designer shows. Good design must come from your heart, from your life experience. Most Chinese designs are too superficial. A good designer must understand the fabric. I mean, fabric has life in the designers' eyes. Many designers today don't know anything about fabric or tailoring, but they think they can become a master someday.

What is the major challenge of building a designer brand in China?

We need professional managers, professional buyers, professional journalists. In general, professionals in all areas of the fashion industry.

What is your dream?

My dream is to be a great designer, then to be a pioneer who penetrates the designer brands market in the international market.

Following is a written interview done after Frankie completed his fifth show in Paris in February 2009.

After parading in Paris Fashion Week for two years running, is there any difference from the first time to the latest one?

The first difference may be the value of 'the first' [China brand to present in Paris Fashion Week]—when I was invited to present at the Paris Fashion Week in 2006. It was the first China brand show as well as the opening show of the 2007 Spring/Summer of Paris Fashion Week. There were a lot of expectations and pressures. After the first time, focus was moved to the product lines. The line needs to be innovative to give a fresh look every season.

After obtaining experience from Paris in the past couple years, do you think Jefen has any unique personality that attracts the overseas buyers?

Jefen [in China] has been growing for many years. The brand has been attracting attention and support from her loyal customers and people from different industries. Jefen presented at the 2007 Spring/Summer Paris Fashion Week targets women who are more internationalized and trendy. I think the brand will sustain long-term development with the support from her consumers.

Of the interviews you gave after the shows, what were the questions mostly about? From these questions do you see any difference between the focus of the Western media and that of Chinese media?

There was much attention given to Jefen, and at the same time, there were lots of questions about the internationalization of Chinese designers. Maybe because the rise of China in the fashion world has been getting a lot of international attention, the international influence of China is still accelerating.

The media's focus depends on whether they're from a social/cultural background or from the industry. Most international people get the knowledge about China through these type of reports.

What is the general depiction of your design style from the overseas media?

In general my design incorporates the Chinese culture into a Western format. [Compared with other Western brands my brand] is relatively neutral and tangled with a touch of the Oriental spirit. This is because I love and admire the spirit of the Oriental culture, at the same time I absorbed nutrition from the Western classic aesthetics.

Where do you think Jefen needs to improve in order to get into the international market?

Vision and innovation. The successes of many international brands are good references, but everyone is unique and different. [I think] we must improve our innovation capacity if we really want to compete with those international designer brands.

What is the biggest hurdle for Jefen in getting into the international market?

The distribution channels, I think it is a hurdle for any brand that wants to get into the international market.

The line presented in Paris looked quite different from the ones selling in the China market. Why is that?

What we launched in Paris is Jefen by Frankie [instead of Jefen]. Jefen by Frankie is for the younger and trendier set. Compared with Jefen it will be more innovative and vigorous.

What do you perceive will be the future of Jefen after being scrutinized by the international market? What is the goal of Jefen in the next five to ten years? In the international market, some brands would consider inviting international financial groups to join the company in order to expand quickly. Some brands like Chanel prefer an organic growth, and they are still privately owned. What will you choose for Jefen?

I wish Jefen to grow steadily. In the coming five to ten years Jefen will continue a healthy development and consolidate her position in the market. Jefen by Frankie will be gradually pushed to the international market. How we handle its further development will depend on any number of factors.

You once said you felt pessimistic for the prospect of designers. The era of designers is over, because now it is the era of financial groups. Do you still believe the function of designers is shrinking?

I don't think it is as simple as that. In fact the successful designers enjoy respect and cult followings overseas. But the success of these designers should not be taken apart from the strong financial groups behind them. I'm sure designers with great and genuine talents eventually will get opportunities and support, but the over-commercialized environment and the dominance over the mainstream market by the international financial giants sometimes suppress the emergence of new and diversified innovations.

LIU YANG: A DESIGNER WHO 'WAS BORN FOR DESIGN, WILL DIE FOR DESIGN'

Of the prominent fashion designers in China, Liu Yang is the one who most has the temperament of an artist. When he was a teenager in the mid 1980s, he permed his long hair and wore wide-leg denims. His outrageous 'rogue man' attire was controversial, and, combined with his handsomeness, made him an object of fascination to many women.

Yang was born in 1969 and was supposed to be included in the second generation of designers, from an age perspective. But he became famous at a very early age, when he was only about twenty. He first gained attention from the public by sweeping the top three awards of the first China Youth Fashion Design Contest in 1988 and later by presenting a fashion show with his own label name in 1990, which few designers had done before. Yang has been a very popular name since the early 1990s, attributed both to his artist temperament and his talents in design. Yang is an all-functional designer. His designs range from women's and men's lines to children's wear. Yang is also the chief designer for the latest uniforms of Chinese policemen.

PORTFOLIO

Born: in the town of San Menxia, He Nan Province, 1969.

Education: Graduated with a bachelor's degree in Clothing Design from Guang-zhou Institute of Fine Arts, 1987.

Career: Fashion designer and merchandiser, the Guangzhou Silk Importing and Exporting Company, 1987; established the Guangzhou Celebrity Clothing Design Firm, 1991; established Guangzhou Liu Yang Fashion Company, 1993; established Guangzhou Liu Yang Arts Creation Company, Ltd. 1996–present; Design Director, brand Yishion, Guangzhou, 2002–present; now the standing director of Sino–U.S Fashion Council, Vice-chairman of China Fashion Association, Chairman of Guang-dong Fashion Association.

Selected Awards

1988, the first-, second- and third-place winner of the first China Youth Fash-ion Design Contest

1991, Silver Award of Hong Kong Fashion Week

1995, Top Ten Chinese Fashion Designers Award by CHIC

1995, Top Five Chinese Fashion Designer Award by the *Asahi* newspaper

1997, World Young Fashion Designer of Excellence Award by *Elle*

1998, Golden Fashion Designer Award by China Fashion Week,

1999, Top Ten Youth of Excellence by the municipal government of Guang-zhou

2006, Ambassador of the City of Guangzhou by the municipal government of Guangzhou

Selected Public Commendations

Do you know in China there is a fashion designer who had to use policemen to escort him from the swarming crowds? Have you heard the story about the passer-by who left his bicycle on the street just to take a look at the star designer? This happened to Liu Yang when he was 28. (Li 1994: 28)

Liu Yang's artwork reveals why his artistic temperament has been attracting a bunch of young Chinese students to commit their lives to fashion design. Yang used his sharp avant-garde design spirit to shock people's eyes and ears and was flattered by the public response. Every time I saw him designing and preparing for the tradeshow for days and nights, often forgetting to eat, exhausted but earnest, I sort of understand why he is regarded as a crucial figure in the industry. (Li and Mao 2006: 5)

Selected International Exposure

1993, Chief Clothing Designer, Closing Ceremony for the Southeast Asian Games

1996, paraded at Leipzig Fashion Trade Fair, Leipzig, Germany

Figure 2.46 Liu Yang (left) with his models, 2005.
Photographer: Feng Hai.

Figure 2.47 Liu Yang with local celebrity stars, 2005.
Photographer: Yang Li.

1999, paraded at Sino–France Cultural Week, Paris
2008, the Visual Communication Senior Consultant for the Sixteenth Asia
Games

Brand: Yishion

Yishion, established in 1997, is one of the largest casual wear brands in China. It has more than 3,000 shops nationwide, most of which are franchises. Yishion also sells in Southeast Asia, the Middle East and Europe. By the time of this interview its total turnover was estimated to be more than 2 billion RMB per year.

Liu Yang was appointed Senior Designer Director for Yishion in 2002.

BIOGRAPHY

'To be or not to be' is how Liu Yang perceives design in his life. He lives and breathes fashion design and cannot imagine doing anything else. His close friend Wang Xin-Yuan, also a fashion designer, once said Yang was 'born for design and will die for design'.

Born for Design (Prior to 1987)

Liu Yang was born during the Cultural Revolution. His family had been exiled and lived in a remote and isolated town called San Menxia, which is next to the ancient city of Luo Yang in He Nan province. The house they lived in for more than a decade after he was born was in fact a cave dwelling.

Although living in extreme poverty Yang was fortunate enough to inherit the artistic gene from his grandfather, who had studied fine arts in France before the liberation, and Liu's mother, a beautiful woman who enjoyed singing and dancing. As soon as Yang was old enough, his mother began teaching him to sing, to paint and to read. Yang's family had a manual sewing machine. He learned sewing when he was only seven. His first achievement was to take his mother's only wedding gift—a red scarf—and transform it into a short pant. Later he stole his father's military uniform trousers and converted them, upside down, to a pair of flare-leg trousers by imitating what he saw in a movie.

Inventing new clothes by modifying old ones became his hobby, and he was often seen wearing his 'new' attire. He was so indulged in his flamboyant appearance by

Figure 2.48 The 2008 Fall/Winter casual line of Yishion.
Photographer: Wei Bin.

Figure 2.49 The 2008 Fall/Winter casual line of Yishion.
Photographer: Wei Bin.

Figure 2.50 The 2006 high fashion line of Yishion.
Photographer: Chen Xu Ren Ren.

Figure 2.51 The 2006 high fashion line of Yishion.
Photographer: Chen Xu Ren Ren.

Figure 2.52 The 2006 high fashion line of Yishion.
Photographer: Yang Li.

his family that townspeople perceived him as a wild rogue, a bad boy. In school, students were asked to cut their hair short and to wear loose straight-cut trousers. Obviously Liu Yang was an exception. Gossip about his appearance didn't bother him. His mother was his strongest supporter, greatly admiring his creativity. She was likely the only person who understood her little boy's talents. She believed her son was a good boy—he always got high scores in school, and liked to help others. He just had a penchant for extravagant looks.

In 1984, at the age of fifteen, he took the entrance exam to university and was admitted to the Guangzhou Institute of Fine Arts. Normally children are supposed to go to school at seven or eight years of age. In the late 1960s and early 1970s, families in remote areas sent their children to schools when the children were only four or five years old, either because there were no kindergartens nearby or parents just wanted their children to start their education earlier. Yang was sent to school when he was four because his father wanted someone to keep an eye on his naughty boy. Except for his mother, no one considered his prospects good, since clothing designers were regarded as little more than tailors even in the 1980s.

Die for Design (1987–1999)

Liu Yang retained his outrageous look during his four years in college. He curled his shoulder-length hair and dyed it blond. He was still an outstanding student, gentle and helpful. He was even asked to join the Community Party—provided he changed his appearance to a more conservative one. He rejected the kind invitation. Although tempted, he wasn't willing to sacrifice his freedom to dress his own way in exchange for having his bad boy status whitewashed.

Despite distinguishing himself in school, he did not know if he was a good designer. Like many of other students in his generation, the first job he got was working in a state-owned company: Guangzhou Silk Importing and Exporting Company. He was given the title of designer, but the work was more like merchandising instead of designing. After he swept the top three prizes in a national fashion designers contest in 1988, he finally proved to himself that he had talent in design.

The dull life in the state-owned company finally drove him to abandon the job. He wanted to start his own business, like the international designers. He had read books about them and to be like them was his dream. His strategy for success began with a catwalk show that would bring fame to both himself and his new company. It was definitely an ambitious plan, because few designers could afford the expense. The budget was approximately 80,000 RMB, at the time, and Liu Yang's monthly income was only 125 RMB.

In a ten-square-meter room near a dilapidated graveyard, Liu Yang started on his grand plan. All he had in the room were a bed, a sewing machine, fabrics and sewing materials. To earn enough money for the show, he made clothes in the evening, then sold them on the streets the next day. In the 1980s and early 1990s, the Chinese favored Western clothing. Many Chinese venders copied the Western labels to mislead people into believing their products were of Western origin. Liu Yang played the same game with his clothes. To sell on the streets was very popular at the time because vendors could neither afford to open a retail shop nor pay the taxes. But it was a high-risk endeavor because the policemen patrolling the area might catch the illegal venders and jail them. But to Liu Yang, it was the best way to earn money quickly.

Eventually, a friend of his provided a free space for his show. Together with the savings from his parents and money he had earned, Liu Yang made his debut in the Dong Fang (Oriental) Hotel in Guangzhou in 1990. His painstaking work was finally rewarded by the success of this show.

That success brought the fame that Liu Yang desired, but it also had a debilitating effect on his health. In order to save money for clothing materials, he had cut his three meals a day to one, or even none, figuring he could 'save a piece of bread for a button'. Right after the show he ended up in the hospital with a gastric hemorrhage that almost killed him.

However, the catwalk show in the hotel had inspired some astute businessmen. They rented clothes from Liu Yang and put on fashion shows as part of the entertainment for hotel and restaurant guests. This unexpected windfall increased his wealth.

Figure 2.53 The artwork of Liu Yang created in 1990.
Photographer: Ren Ping.

He finally bought a house and car in Guangzhou when the majority of Chinese people were still making meagre wages and striving for three meals a day. Liu Yang had finally realized his dream of becoming a star in China's fashion world.

It is worth noting that before Liu Yang became a well-known designer in China, clothing designers were normally regarded as little more than tailors. When pictures of the handsome and athletic Liu Yang appeared in magazines and newspapers, he attracted hordes of fascinated fans. The media said he had 'bridged the gap between tailor and star', likening him to a singer or film star. His fans followed him and swarmed around him once he was seen in public; sometimes police had to escort him through the streets.

Life under the bright light of his star was enjoyable, but then tragedy struck like lightning. His business partner stripped the company account and disappeared. Liu Yang became bankrupt overnight. He had to sell his house and car and return to an ordinary life. The instant drop from the top of the heap to the bottom was embarrassing for the flambouyant designer. He had to take public buses instead of limousines. He wore dark sun-glasses to ensure nobody recognized him. If someone did recognize him, he explained he was trying a different lifestyle as a designer.

In 1996, Liu Yang was invited by the government of Germany to present at the Leipzig Fashion Fair. Germany searched around for a stereotypical Asian fashion designer, and Yang was recommended. The organizer made a commitment to pay all his travel and parade expenses except for the clothes. Liu Yang was treated like royalty in Leipzig, with lodgings in a five-star hotel, and a luxury car at his disposal.

However, when Liu Yang entered the show hall before the parade started, he was shocked by a brazen display of monochromatic photographs taken in China— a group of sloppy little girls and boys with runny noses sitting in front of a dilapidated house; a group of men seated at a table and eating live animals like monkeys or ants; colourful underwear hanging on clotheslines outside the houses. Perhaps the organizer merely wanted to show the daily lives of Chinese people, but the primitiveness and backwardness displayed in the photos offended Liu Yang. How could they show such negative images when there was so much in China that was beautiful? Liu Yang demanded that all the pictures be taken down or he would refuse to present the show. The organizer responded that he would be sued for millions under breach of contract. The Germans did not understand that to Liu Yang the issue was as serious as a political crisis. He expected his show to be an icon, one that honored his country and countrymen. He even warned the organizer that he would cut his clothes to pieces if the organizer refused to take down the offensive pictures. Two minutes before the show, all the pictures were taken from the walls.

The show received great acclaim from the public. People lined up to get his autograph. They loved Liu Yang's splendid evening dresses. The Minister of Economy said, 'I will have to re-evaluate Chinese people,' and 'We should not ignore our competitors from the Far East.'

By the show's end, Liu Yang received the distinction and honor he so richly deserved, though it was tainted with the controversy surrounding the pictures as well as his negative experience in a local restaurant. Prior to the show, Liu Yang had had lunch with friends in a local restaurant. The waitresses ignored Yang and his guests and only served local people. Liu Yang went back to the restaurant the next day, after the show, and this time his waitress served him with a big smile. Obviously she had read the newspaper headlines and discovered he was a famous fashion designer.

When he returned home from the show, Liu Yang was back on top again. He worked with local clothing manufacturers, mostly helping them organize shows, since these manufacturers needed Liu's name to attract media for their brand fashion shows. However, as other designers had discovered, Liu realized that marriage with local fashion enterprises was doomed to failure. Henceforth, he limited himself to presenting catwalk shows.

Figure 2.54 Liu Yang with the then-mayor of Leipzig, 1996.
Photographer: Ren Ping.

Re-birth: Lifestyle Designer (2000–)

The long hours and hard work took a toll on Liu Yang's body. The shows burned him out, taking so much energy that he was often sent to the hospital before or after a show. To achieve perfection, he oftentimes asked his assistants to bring their laptops to the hospital where he could guide them in making improvements in design.

Although he achieved his goals in reputation as well as financial security, he was tired in body and heart. He immigrated to New York in 1999. 'I feel in past years I was like a non-stop machine. All my life was about fame and career. I felt exhausted. More important, even though I had gained fame and money, I didn't feel happy.'

New York changed his outlook on life. 'For the first time I knew what life was about. There are so many things you can enjoy in this world other than work. The sunshine, the clean air, the beach, sex, friendship, Broadway, dancing…I never felt so happy as when I lay on a bench in Central Park with a hamburger in one hand and a Coke in the other.'

The leisurely lifestyle in New York did not deter Liu Yang from his dream of being a great designer, but it gave him a different perspective. He realized he had been in a superficial world before, and now it was time to get down to earth. He visited local artists and gained inspiration from them. He visited local museums and shops, always thinking about how he could get into the international market. Fame was as fragile as a bubble, but one day a chance encounter with a young boy showed him what his dream should be. Yang asked the boy what clothes he wanted to wear when he grew up. The boy answered, 'My father's Armani jacket'. Yang realized that what Armani sold was a lifestyle, a culture, and that is what his own goal should be—a professional international fashion designer.

Living in New York was good for Liu Yang. It gave him time to think about his life and what kind of designer he wanted to be.

He lived in New York for only a few years, but returned to China every year to present at China Fashion Week. While there, he refused media interviews. 'I wanted to prove that I was not any more a designer who cares more about fame. I do it just because I love what I am doing. Now I am more grounded.' Life in New York also injected new blood in his design. To the Liu Yang of today, life is more than design, design is more than just making clothes. To have a healthy body and live more peacefully has become his life philosophy.

Partnership with Yishion (2002–)

Yang had been working with several Chinese giant enterprises before he partnered with the company of Yishion. Early on, the partnership failed to succeed because 'neither of the parties had experience.' In 2002 Yishion contracted with Yang and appointed him the Senior Design Director of the brand. The owner of the business was young and diligent, as well as open-minded. Yang was given sufficient authority and power to develop the collection. The dependable relationship eventually made Yishion one of the largest causal clothing brands in China.

Figure 2.55 Line designed by Liu Yang for the brand Sidima, 2001. Photographer: Juan Zi.

Figure 2.56 Line designed by Liu Yang for a local brand, 2001.
Photographer: Juan Zi.

Figure 2.57 Line designed by Liu Yang for a local brand, 2001.
Photographer: Juan Zi.

Figure 2.58 Line designed by Liu Yang for a local brand, 2001.
Photographer: Juan Zi.

Figure 2.59 The 'Dancing with Wolf' show directed by
Liu Yang for local men's wear brand Sept Wolf in 1998.
Photographer: Ji Mi.

DIALOGUE

What do you want people to say about you when one day you retire from
the fashion stage?

I hope people would say, 'He is a good, professional designer.'

Figure 2.60 Liu Yang's design for local men's wear brand
Faboer, 2005. Photographer: Tu Wen-An.

Figure 2.61 Liu Yang's design for local men's wear brand
Faboer, 2005. Photographer: Tu Wen-An.

Figure 2.62 Liu Yang's design for local men's wear brand
Faboer, 2005. Photographer: Tu Wen-An.

From where do you get inspirations for your collection every season?

Life experience. It can be anything in your life.

As a fashion designer, what is your biggest challenge today? And what was your biggest challenge when you first started your business?

In terms of the external factor, it should be capital support. Plus a good entrepreneur who understands design. As for myself I think the challenge is to keep exceeding myself.

How do you recruit a designer?

I care very much if the candidate is filial to his or her parents. I think if he is nice to his parents he can be friendly to other people. This is hard to judge by one time interview. But if I found the person is not the right one, I educate him first, and if he still doesn't change, I fire him. In terms of design, the portfolio is the first thing I would see. I would also ask him what the trend is today. And who he admires (not John Galliano). Many students tell me how much they admire John Galliano, but there are many outstanding designers in the world who are worthy of our respect. John Galliano is just a lucky man. He is fortunate enough...

What is your ultimate goal?

Build my own high fashion brand—Liu Yang. I'm the one who started the made-to-measure couture business in the early days in China.

Do you have any Western designers that you admire?

I mostly admire those from older times: Chanel, Madame Chanel's design, Dior, Pierre Cardin, Ungaro, Givenchy, I like his noble temperament. Karl Lagerfeld, but before he lost his weight. He now looks eccentric to me. Dolce & Gabana—I'm fascinated by their avant-garde style.

Have you had any communication with any Western fashion designers? In your view, what are the major differences between Chinese fashion designers and Western designers?

A true master is very vigorous. They seem to always have enough energy to do all the work. They are also very humble. Compared to them I think Chinese designers easily go to extremes, either haughty or feeling inferior. Many of our younger Chinese designers are easily getting puffed up by their own consequence, but they don't even know fabric and zippers.

When was the first time you went abroad? Where was it? And how did you feel about the trip?

1988, Hong Kong. They all thought I was from Taiwan, because of my modern look. I felt quite flattered at the time. You know, many Chinese people were labeled as mainland Chinese by their attire when they went abroad in the 1980s and 1990s. I was very impressed by their civilization—people were all very polite and in neat and nice clothes, the air was clean, there were many skyscrapers...

What made you choose Guangzhou?

I love design, I love art. I chose Guangzhou because it was the most open city in China in the 1980s. I love her tolerance. I wanted to be famous, be known by many people. I wanted to be a star. Because I was born in a poor family, and I thought fame would bring money to me, improve our quality of life. And I thought I had the talent to become a star.

What do you think of those who criticize you?

People thought I made lots of money by working for those manufacturers, and they think I only know how to present a show (instead of making profits for the manufacturers). As a matter of fact sometimes I even paid money out of my own pocket when working for the companies. I paid my own travel expenses and never asked for reimbursement from the company. You know to be or not to be, I love design, it is as simple as that, not for the money. I want to be the best. I have been criticized since I was a young kid, firstly because of the way I dressed, then because of my shows. Sometimes the words even interfered with my life. People thought I was homosexual because of the way I dressed and how I talked, but as a matter of fact I am a normal man, just like most men. I am not against gays, but I don't think people should criticize based on what they can only guess at. I used to care what people said about me, but now I live for myself and to contribute as much as I can to the design industry.

Fortunately people are more tolerant and open-minded nowadays. I think time will tell. People now, including the media, appreciate my profession and they know I'm actually a grounded person instead of a superficial one. My seven-year partnership with Yishion is a good example—I can bring value to enterprise. I can devote my life to design and arts. I'm just a person enchanted by the beauty in life. I don't mind being misunderstood and I believe time will prove many things.

THE FIRST GENERATION OF CHINESE DESIGNERS: A GENERATION FEATURING 'CHINESE'

The growth experience of these four designers represents the essence of their generation. They were all born between 1950–1960, had done varied jobs, experienced different political movements prior to their design careers, and thus possessed a strong knowledge of politics and an ability to bear hardships. They obtained their design skills from the institutions, creating in them a natural affinity for schools that eventually led them to be educators and coaches when their commercial enterprises were unsuccessful. They had enormous passion for fashion and art, though their inspirational reservoir came mostly from the historical costumes of China. They have experienced the ups and downs in life as well as the praise and criticisms in their careers, and finally, a few of them achieved prominence in the industry.

These four designers epitomize the best of their generation. Xin-Yuan assumed a position in the fashion federation and also consults on different design projects—not only clothing design, but also interior design and landscape design. Hai-Yan teaches in school and is an outstanding professor in academic circles, while at the same time, she provides design consultancy services in her WHY studio. Hai-Yan is a member of the National Committee of the Chinese People's Political Consultative Conference, a title of high social responsibility. Yang works for a clothing company and also teaches in college and consults on design projects. At the same time he is providing made-to-measure service to celebrities. Frankie Xie, probably the most blessed of them all, designs and sells his own labels.

During the interviews, the conversations with the four designers featured a blend of emotions: happiness, excitement, pride, sadness, frustration and sorrow. After all, the heart's desire of most designers is to have a label with his or her name on it—something few of them have achieved. When the first generation of designers turns fifty, who knows how many of them will still hold firm to their dreams...

Looking back, success was destined to elude the first generation, post-Mao, because the environment in the 1980s was not favorable to designers.

Reviewing the emergence and development of Western designers provides a better approach to studying the general failure of the first generation of Chinese fashion designers.

In the Western world, designers—creators of clothing design—did not become an apparent profession until the 1960s. But prior to that, the development of nearly 200 years of cutting techniques and approximately 100 years of couture houses certainly founded a concrete base for the emergence of the new clothing creators.

The various sumptuous costumes created throughout history provided inspirational sources for these young designers. Many of the influential designers after World War II came from the couture houses: Gabrielle Chanel and Yves Saint Laurent are probably the names easiest to recognize.

A changing social environment was another factor that favored the growth of fashion design. In 1920 the women's emancipation movement encouraged Gabrielle Chanel to create her Chanel-style suits in the 1920s and 1930s. In the 1940s the shortage of materials due to World War II led Christian Dior to create his 'new look' that became popular overnight. By the 1960s the rebellious youth movement made Mary Quant's mini-skirt a new star. In the 1960s, the growth of the baby boom generation created new needs for ready-to-wear clothes, offering mass-market pricing with a taste of modernity and personality. Haute couture was out of mode and too expensive for the younger generation.

We should not neglect the influence of artists and movie stars. For instance, Mondrian's paintings were adopted by Yves Saint Laurent for his designs, the pieces becoming one of the signatures of YSL; Jean Paul Gautier earned international fame when Madonna wore his cone-bra at her Truth or Dare concerts.

Last but not least, capital backing is critical to the development of any commercial endeavor. The economic boom after World War II created a 'need' for new and beautiful clothing, as well as the ability to afford them. This new, affluent environment promoted the emergence and development of fashion designers.

However, a strong political cast still dominated China in the 1980s. The legacy ideology regarded outfits as mirrors of the wearers' political identification. Few people were brave enough to wear fashionable clothes for fear they would be regarded as subversive.

With regard to the socio-cultural aspect, wearing clothes was more a utilitarian necessity, not an opportunity for an aesthetic display. The utilitarian philosophy dates back to China's early history. To traditional Chinese, only concrete, practical and functional articles are worthy of investment. In schools as well as at home, children were taught that frugality was a traditional virtue of Chinese people. Money should only be used for utilitarian needs at the least cost. This also explains why artistic items such as paintings are not as popular in China as they are in the Western world.

The overall economic climate in China in the 1980s restricted the number of people who could afford fashionable clothes. Even after the transition from isolation to an open-door policy, only a small group of people—mostly the first generation of revolutionists—gained affluence. They sported Western clothing as an indication of their financial status, and this led them to pay for fake Western labels that they thought were luxury goods. Not until the late 1990s did this first generation of rich people discover that these so-called luxury goods were, in fact, fakes. On the other end, those with meager incomes could only afford to buy cheap, mass-produced clothes.

The overall clothing industry in the 1980s was on the verge of transformation. However, lack of knowledge and experience, anxiety about achieving success, isolation from the world beyond China, and the inexplicable megalomania eventually led the industry to place the focus on the wrong facets.

The various industrial associations and committees mostly engaged in all kinds of fashion festivals and used the designers to promote both the designers and organizations. Contests were the mainstay, basically the sole channels for discovering new designer stars. Theatrical shows were used to promote the designers. Compared to their Western counterparts, the Chinese organizations made little effort to help designers in the aspects of commerce, such as doing fund raising for young talents, providing professional consultancy and mentoring to start-up designer ventures and bridging the design talents with business units. The market isolation turned fashion festivals into entertainment programs rather than platforms to deliver trend information to the professionals and the masses. This eventually led the early designers to be just show designers. The show designers earned fame, but little profit.

Enterprises and/or entrepreneurs were another force deciding the destiny of designers. In the West, in the early days, Chanel had her mythical lover who supported her in opening her first shop; without Pierre Berge, Yves Saint Laurent might not have achieved the pinnacle of his career. In recent years, Domenico De Sole and Tom Ford partnered and revived the business of Gucci; with Bernard Arnauld's support Marc Jacob, John Galliano and Michael Kors burst on the international scene. Chinese entrepreneurs and Chinese fashion designers tried to partner on the same model. However, the Chinese partners learned the format but not the spirit of a successful partnership.

The first generation of Chinese entrepreneurs—in general less informed—mostly obtained their fortunes quickly through manufacturing and wholesaling garments, expecting the designers to be the saviors of their brands as they noticed the emergence of the domestic market. They had neither knowledge in the mysteries of brand building nor patience with the slow growth of sales numbers. Compared with manufacturing and wholesaling, branding needs a longer time to grow. In the 1980s and 1990s, a popular format adopted for brand building was to recruit a famous designer and hire a celebrity to advertise everywhere for the brand, together with an expensive shop display. This format still prevails for new brands in most areas of China. And it worked quite well for some of the mass-market brands. It is certainly not fair to say the entrepreneurs did not invest enough money on the branding. But when the investment was not returned proportionally, the companies placed all the blame on the designers. Designers often talked about the interference from their business partners, such as stepping into the designer's studio and changing some aspect of the clothing design, believing they knew what would sell and what would not sell. To a certain degree, this is true. However, who is supposed to be responsible for the design, then? Another phenomenon worthy of note is that almost all the interviewed designers had been stripped of their property by their business partners. Many designers of the first generation attributed the failure of their business to their naivety in looking for appropriate partners.

A developing industry should not neglect its education. The unique teaching methodology in China created a group of very 'Chinese' designers. Somehow its fashion design courses were mistranslated into the equivalent of fashion illustration from the very beginning. But given the fact that the country was in general isolated from the outside world, and the first generation fashion educators basically explored the syllabuses by themselves, they certainly deserve more respect and understanding than criticism. The fact is many students were attracted to the courses because of a passion for painting rather than clothing design. The two subjects may not necessarily contradict each other, and some of the students eventually discovered that fashion can be fascinating too. But in general it misled students about the concept of fashion design. Young graduate designers normally conceived the clothes on a flat plane, since their works were mostly drawn on paper. In addition, the split between fashion design and fashion engineering courses meant the designers and pattern cutters had no common language. The most common criticism is lack of practical skills.

Synchronized collaboration is critical to the development of the industry. Western fashion designers liaise with public relations agencies, sales agencies, buyers, journalists and textile millers. The big names are backed by a team of professionals in all aspects. The first generation of Chinese designers acted as lonely warriors, because they had to do all the work themselves due to the general backwardness of the industry at the time. A common issue was the difficulty in finding high-quality fabrics and exquisite accessories. Most factories produced products for mass-market use. The other common challenge was finding qualified sales agencies and trying to get into the department stores. The designers often found themselves involved in everything but design.

Brevity, innovation, diligence and intelligence are the engines driving designers towards their goals. The three legendary Japanese designers—Rei Kawakubo, Issey Miyake and Yohji Yamamoto best exemplify this category. They shocked the Western design world with the loose form that emancipated women's bodies. Their new design philosophy challenged the traditional definition of beauty in the West and provided a totally different approach from an Asian perspective.

The first generation of Chinese designers certainly has brevity and diligence. At the same time, from the interviews and the examples of the designers, it can be concluded that the design philosophy of the first generation carries the strong hall-mark of their times.

The first impression was how much this generation underscored their Chinese identification. They believe in the philosophy of 'the national is the international'. They spent a lot of time studying historical Chinese culture and artefacts, and transformed the heritage to a modern interpretation, then applied it to their clothes. The rationale behind such a philosophy might be that as designers they needed to distinguish their styles from those in the West. The result is that 'Chinese' elements became their choice. In addition, these Chinese elements are exotic to most of the Western world, such features providing a fresh look. Another factor is their childhood education in patriotism. The spirit of patriotism especially left a strong mark on the first generation due to all the political movements and events they experienced.

Another signature of the first generation of Chinese designers is their use of the classic elegance of the 1920s to the 1950s that European couturiers had adopted. Clothes were proportionally balanced and cutting lines were traditionally placed in position. Their creativity was evident in the special fabrics, prints, embroideries, subtle variations of collars, pockets and buttons and many other details. In general, these things look quite traditional from today's perspective, but relating the phenomenon with their growth experience shows that this can be linked to their early influences. Pierre Cardin, Yves Saint Laurent, Madame Chanel and Christian Dior were the first big-name designers known by the Chinese designers. Imitating these big-name designers' styles became an easy way of starting out for these Chinese pioneers.

What deserves attention is their philosophical way of thinking. The numerous ups and downs in their lives trained them to behave more like philosophers than designers. Their value systems affected the way they perceived and created design. For instance, they believed the function of the clothes was more important than creativity. An article of clothing that looks innovative but isn't practical was not considered good design. Being pragmatic and beautiful (in a traditional concept), instead of being creative or unique, is usually how they approached a new design piece (though not the pieces designed for shows).

When Chinese fashion debuted in Paris in 1987, people started to make predictions about when China would have her own master designers like Pierre Cardin, and who would be the ones to succeed. The guessing game is still going strong more than twenty years later.

Whenever Chinese designers parade in Western countries, the fashion industry shows a burst of excitement. Unfortunately, many Chinese fashion designers don't fully understand the international branding game, thinking that participation in the international parades will help them get into the international market. In fact, most of the parades, except for the most recent ones, were either for entertainment or for a cultural exchange instead of for commercial purposes. The applause and commendation from the Western media was likely out of courtesy, as well as curiosity about exotic cultures, rather than an appreciation of commercial values.

The flowers and applause did not bring them the commercial success they hoped for, but these Chinese design pioneers certainly deserved the compliments they received, like 'versatile', 'daring', 'adventurous' and 'respectful'. The rise of the new clothing design profession has been capturing the fancy of many young people, but it comes with a harsh dose of reality. Once in, these young designers find that the profession is like any other commercial enterprise, where talent alone is no guarantee to superstardom. To produce a label that will be successful in the marketplace, one also needs strong financial backing, a savvy business partner and collaboration with other parties. Translating design talent to market value is a complex process. The Chinese fashion designers who emerged in the 1980s were in a much more complicated and challenging environment and deserve commendation instead of criticism. They paved the way for those who followed and contributed greatly to the development of the Chinese fashion design industry. Designers like Frankie Xie (although an exception in his generation) shone a light on the future of the Chinese designers. Kudos to the pioneers!

3 THE 1990s: THE SECOND GENERATION—PRACTITIONERS

BACKGROUND
SOCIO-ECONOMIC CONDITIONS

By the beginning of the1990s, the political environment in China was becoming more relaxed. Debate over whether developing the nation's economy was equivalent to capitalism finally came to a conclusion when the then-helmsman of the country, Deng Xiao-Ping, proposed the development of the Socialist Market Economy[1]. The Socialist Market Economy system gradually replaced the Planned Economic System, paving the way for the emergence of private companies, joint ventures and foreigner-invested companies—realms that were previously occupied by state-owned companies.

The Chinese people were more open-mind in the 1990s than they were in the 1980s. Clothing choices were no longer regarded as a political statement. More variety in wearing apparel was offered, including authentic international brands. In April 1992, Louise Vuitton opened a flagship store in the nation's top five-star hotel: Beijing Wang Fu Jing Grand Hotel. Luxury brands by Armani, Chanel, Gucci and Dior followed, foreshadowing the emergence of a new breed of customer in China. However, at the time, luxury brands could only be purchased by FEC[2], and therefore were still restricted to a small group of people. Regardless, trendy Chinese women began to dye their hair, wear mini-skirts and see-through shirts, and experiment with body piercing.

THE FASHION INDUSTRY

In 1995, a strategic development plan called Famous Label Strategy was initiated by Dong Bin-Gen, General Manager of China Garment Group, at the conference of Strategic Development Plan of Clothing Industry in China. The speech was later enlarged upon by Du Yu-Zhou, Vice-president of China Textile Association, to affirm the development of local famous labels in China. Adventurous groups of individuals established their own private companies in the wake of the economic reform. Labels like Lining, now the most successful sports brand in China; Meters Bownwe, the largest casual-wear label in China; and White Collar, one of the top-selling labels in businesswomen's attire, were all founded in the beginning and the mid 1990s.

In the meantime, some designers viewed the Famous Label Strategy as a prelude to a more exuberant evolution. They foresaw the potential market available in the nation's prodigious population. Designer labels like Exception by Ma Ke, Tangy by Liang Zi and Omnialuo by Luo Zhen were the new breed born with the new economy strategy.

Fashion Models

For the first time in 1991, China became one of the contest regions of the Supermodel of the World Contest. Chen Juan-Hong was the winner for the China Region.

In 1992, Chen Juan-Hong won the title of World Super Model in the United States.

In 1996, the National Textile Association and Ministry of Labor jointly issued the Professional Fashion Model Standards. 'Fashion Model' was finally recognized as a profession by the Chinese government.

Fashion Magazines

The international fashion magazine *Cosmopolitan* landed in China through a partnership with *Fashion* magazine in 1998.

Fashion Trade Fairs

In May 1993, the first CHIC clothing trade fair was hosted in Beijing. Three distinguished designers—Valentino Garavani, Gianfranco Ferre and Pierre Cardin—participated. Now CHIC is the largest clothing trade fair in China.

In 1997, the first Chinese Designers Expo was held in Beijing. The Expo launched the presentation of 'Golden Awards' to top local fashion designers. The Expo name was later changed to China Fashion Week, now China International Fashion Week.

The Industrial Association

In October 1998, the China Fashion Association (CFA) was founded. The organization was created especially for the promotion of local designers and designer brands. It is also the host of the then-China Fashion Week and now China International Fashion Week.

Fashion Design Contest

In May 1993, the first international fashion design contest in China, the Brother Cup, was held in Beijing.

Exposure Overseas

In 1998, a catwalk show bearing the theme 'Chinese Historical Costume' was presented in the Louvre Museum, Paris.

Fashion Education

The first international design school, Lasaer International Design Institute (now the Raffles International Design Institute), was established in 1994in Shanghai through a joint partnership with Dong Hua University.

LIANG ZI: A HARMONIOUS DESIGNER

Liang Zi was among the first designers to start her own label in the mid 1990s. Her label, Tangy, was established in 1994. The brand, featuring a blend of Chinese spirit and modern taste, now generates more than 200 million RMB in revenue every year.

PORTFOLIO

Original Name: Liang Yi-Hong.

Born: in a small town near the city of Shaoxing, Zhejiang Province, 1965. Now based in the city of Shenzhen, Guangdong Province.

Education: Received training certificate in pattern cutting at the Zhejiang Institute of Silk Science, Zhejiang Province, 1984; Graduated with a bachelor's degree in fashion design from the Northwest Institute of Textile Engineering, Shaan Xi Province, 1990; received training certificate in modelling from the Chambre Syndicale De La Couture Paris School, Paris, 1999; received short-course certificate in fashion design from the Fashion Institute of Technology, New York, 2001.

Career: cutter and designer, Hangzhou Xidebao Travelling Goods Co., Zhejiang Province, 1990–1992; designer, Zhejiang Silk Importing & Exporting Group, Shenzhen regional office, Guangdong Province, 1992–1994; formed her own brand, Tangy, in Shenzhen, Guangdong Province, 1994; presented at Seoul Fashion Week, Korea, 2002; presented at the show of China Fashion organized by the China Fashion

Association, Paris, 2003; presented at the Shanghai International Fashion Festival, 2005; presented at Kuala Lumpur Fashion Week, Malaysia, 2005.

Selected Awards

2001, Top Ten Fashion Designers Award by China Fashion Week

2004, 2005, Best Womenswear Designer Award and Best Womenswear Brand Award by China Fashion Week

2005, Top Ten National Excellence of Young Designers Award, co-organized by China Architects' Association, China Industrial Products Designers' Association and China Fashion Designers' Association

Selected Public Commendations

The Golden Award, the best award for Chinese fashion designers, led Liang Zi, a perfectionist, to strive for it for ten years. From a worker in a garment factory to a machinist in a college, from a merchandiser to sales clerk to chief designer and deputy general manager, until today when she is standing on the top tier of Chinese fashion designers, Liang Zi's passion for nature never wavered. She continuously shows her peace, health, beauty and enthusiasm for life lyrically. (Jewel 2008: 150)

Liang Zi is the environmental protector in the fashion world. As the fashion designer, she received the top award, the Golden Award, and the Best Womenswear Designer Award. As the environmental protector, she discovered and protected the Chinese precious traditional fabric *Shu Liang* Silk, and transformed the 500-year-old silk into the sumptuous and delicate costumes shown in the Museum Louvre in Paris. (Liu 2008: B36)

Brand: Tangy

Tangy was founded in 1994 by Liang Zi, the chief designer, and her husband Huang Zhi-Hua, the general manager of the company. *Tangy* means 'nature, human into one' in Chinese. Adhering to the principles of peace, health and beauty, Tangy only uses natural fibres like cotton, silk and linen, which are also traditional Chinese fabrics. Designs are simple and mostly straight-cut in form, combined with intricate floral embroidery in contrasting colours. Viewed from a distance, Tangy dresses are more like Chinese oil paintings. All the clothes present a consideration for peace, harmony and health, blended with a simple contemporary flavour and bold colours.

Figure 3.1 Liang Zi with models at China International Fashion Week in 2003. Photographer: Yu Jian.

Tangy includes lines for men and women that sell in the hundreds of RMB, but has no defined ages for target consumers. There are more than 350 shops all over the country, most operated through franchises, with annual revenues of more than 200 million RMB in 2008. Tangy is one of the largest Chinese designer brands in China today.

BIOGRAPHY

Liang Zi may not be the most beautiful woman in China, but she certainly is a woman who presents the most harmonious appeal. Speaking in a gentle, soft voice, Liang Zi nonetheless packs her passion for fashion design into a calm but firm faith in her future.

From Rural Countryside to Fashion School (Prior to 1990)

As a teenager, Liang Zi showed an unusual interest in clothes. Each year when receiving a new article of clothing from her mother as a new year's gift, she always went to a tailor's shop and instructed the tailor to alter the clothes. She wanted to look different than the other girls. She did not realize her enthusiasm came from her fashion design flair because fashion was still taboo in her childhood.

Liang Zi finished high school at fourteen, an age too young to get into college, so she went to a local tailor's shop to be an apprentice. One month later, she left—the tailor told her she was skilful enough to make clothes on her own. The apprentice, probably the one with the least training in the world, opened a tailor shop of her own. Shortly thereafter, she was hired by a local garment factory and became a full-time dressmaker.

This self-study mode of tailoring soon ignited her desire to get more formal education to enhance her skills. The small town where she lived was too isolated for her to continue her studies. To improve her cutting skills, she went to Hangzhou, the closest urban city, and enrolled in the men's tailoring class hosted by the Zhejiang Institute of Silk Science. Six months later after successfully passing the final exams of the program, she was hired as a machinist trainer by the school.

Liang Zi first heard the term 'fashion design' when she was working in the school. She thought it was a perfect match for her dream: she liked drawing and she loved making clothes. However, college entrance exams in the 1980s were extremely difficult due to the large number of older students trying to make up for their missed opportunity to study during the Cultural Revolution. Competing with the younger generation to get into the colleges, many of them had been trying to pass the exams for four or five years. Undaunted, Liang Zi decided to take the unified entrance exams at the age of twenty in order to pursue her dream, regardless of the challenges ahead of her.

To afford the expensive textbooks and drawing tools, Liang Zi had to keep working while she prepared for the entrance exams. She worked in the daytime, then took drawing classes in night school. After returning home, she continued to study until midnight each night, leaving little time for sleep. She spent modest sums on food in order to save for tuition. This harsh schedule eventually landed her in the hospital for a month.

But in September 1986 her painstaking work was rewarded with an admission letter from the Northwest Institute of Textile Engineering. Located in the northwest city of Xi An, Shaan Xi Province, the school was one of the first to offer fashion design courses in the 1980s.

While many younger students slacked off after passing the difficult entrance exams, Liang Zi continued to immerse herself in intense study. To earn money for tuition and gain valuable work experience, she again set herself a busy schedule, studying in the daytime and then working part-time in the evening. She graduated with distinction in 1990.

Life in a State-owned Company (1990–1994)

By the time she graduated, the government had stopped matching jobs for college graduates. Graduates had to hunt for jobs themselves. In addition, the national Residence Card[3] system required all students to return to their hometown areas to work after their graduation. Liang Zi found a job in Hangzhou (near her hometown) and worked there for two years as a cutter and designer. She then moved with her husband, Huang Zhi-Hua, who had also been her classmate, to the Shenzhen regional office of Zhejiang Silk Importing & Exporting Group, one of the largest textile and clothing trading companies in China.

Shenzhen is near Hong Kong and one of the first Four Special Economic Zones opened to foreign investors in the 1980s. When the couple arrived in Shenzhen, they were immediately impressed by the energy of the young city. They noticed the emergence of the domestic clothing market and suggested that the state-owned company Zhejiang Silk switch its focus from exporting to the domestic market. However, management was not motivated to start a new venture because of the stable growth of its exporting revenue.

In the state-owned companies, designers spent most of their time duplicating styles from magazines. Liang Zi was just one of them. By the mid 1990s, clothes in most of the shops bore a remarkable sameness. Liang Zi saw this as a prime market opportunity. 'I saw the best-selling dresses in department stores and I thought I could make dresses that were nicer, so I decided to start my own business,' said Liang Zi.

Building a Brand: Tangy (1994–)

With an eight-square-meter freestanding shop in Shenzhen, Liang Zi started her journey as an independent designer. At the time the clothing market was dominated by cheap synthetic fabrics. Liang Zi differentiated her label by using natural fabrics: silk, cotton and linen. The cutting and making skills gained from her past experience proved to be very useful when she started her own label. In the daytime, she acted as a sales clerk in the shop; in the evening, she sketched the designs, then cut and made the clothes. When sales began to soar, she hired a sales assistant for the shop and started to outsource to factories to make the clothes for her. In the meantime, she tried to sell her clothes to the department stores. 'Department stores and factories were the places I visited most often,' Liang Zi said. 'My home was my design studio, packed with patterns and samples. I was always carrying two big packages of fabrics to garment factories or two bags of clothing to department stores, regardless of the weather outside. It was not easy, you know. It is an unforgettable memory in my life.'

The unique designs and the comfort of the fabrics gradually gained a group of loyal customers for Tangy. Many franchises approached Liang Zi offering to distribute her products. The brand became so popular that illegal copies were seen in shops in rural areas.

To expand the business more aggressively, in 2001 Tangy presented its first public show at China Fashion Week in Beijing. Contrasting with the many extravagant and theatrical types of shows, Tangy gave the spectators a spiritual and peaceful vision through its simple, clean-cut lines blended with the natural look of its fabrics. Liang Zi won first place in the competition for Top Ten Fashion Designers of the year. Thereafter Liang Zi has been representing Chinese fashion designers in parades at the fashion weeks in Seoul, Paris and Kuala Lumpur.

Tangy owns more than 350 shops and four factories, with annual turnover in excess of 200 million RMB, making it one of the most successful Chinese designer brands today.

Chinese Roots

Like many other Chinese fashion designers, Liang Zi believes that as a Chinese designer her brand should carry a spirit of 'Chinese'. Since founding the brand, she had been seeking a format that, while still reflecting the Chinese spirit, has the flexibility to be transformed into a modern, trendy statement.

An accidental discovery led Liang Zi to rejuvenate an ancient Chinese textile named *Shu Liang*, a type of fabric that is on the verge of extinction today. *Shu Liang* has existed in Chinese history for more than 500 years. The fabric is first made of silk, then dyed in *Shu Liang* juice, a type of Chinese medicine obtained from the *Shu Liang* plant. This is followed by a long immersion in mineral clay. Both the juice and the mineral clay are only available in a small village in southern China. The fabric needs considerable time to dry in the sun after being dyed, so production is solely limited to sunny days between April and October. Unlike normal silks, *Shu Liang* only has one colour—black on the back side, the colour of the clay, and coffee brown on the face side, the medicinal juice colour. The fabric is anti-bacterial and wrinkle-resistant because no chemical dyes are used. The labour-intensive dying formula has been mastered by a limited number of people. Its geographical and seasonal constraints made it a rare treasure, so that only rich families could afford it.

Liang Zi felt a thrill in her heart when she first saw the ancient fabrics. She revived the lost art, and is now widely regarded as a leader in restoring this Chinese heritage. However, in an age of mass production, legacy fabrics like *Shu Liang* are losing their attraction because of the complexity and high cost in producing them. Acknowledging this fact, and taking advantage of the uniqueness of the fabric, she added a wide spectrum of colours by replacing the medicinal juice with ecological dyes so that she can have more choices in colours for her clothes design. Although the *Shu Liang* collection did not immediately generate profits for Tangy, Liang Zi took it as her responsibility to rejuvenate the ancient textile technology and never compromised her faith in the market. She believed in the long run her customers would fall in love with the fabric. The *Shu Liang* collection became profitable five years after its launch and is now an indispensable part of Tangy.

To honour the legacy of the ancient maritime Silk Road, the Swedish government sent a replica of the Swedish merchant ship, *Goteborg,* to the city of Guangzhou in August 2006. At the request of the Guangzhou government, Liang Zi used *Shu Liang* to design two sets of clothing for the King and the Queen of Sweden as gifts of appreciation from the Chinese government.

A Modern Chinese Private Company

The history of Tangy exemplifies the development of many private companies in China. They normally start as mom-and-pop shops mostly funded from the family savings or loans from friends or relatives. Some of them eventually grow to become large-scale companies worth several hundred million RMB.

When Liang Zi and her husband started their own business, they injected a new management philosophy into the business, based on what they learned from time spent in the state-owned enterprises. For instance, Tangy is one of the successful companies that adopted a franchise model while owning a valuable branding and manufacturing chain. To find good franchisees and sustain them in China is difficult due to the economic and cultural diversity in the country. Financial strength is not the most important factor in becoming a franchisee of Tangy. High on the list of priorities is to share the philosophy of the brand. In addition, the franchisees must maintain the sustainability of the brand—they cannot be short-term profit seekers.

In addition to the daily operational support, the company also provides regular training programs and rewards and rebates to top-performing franchisees. A company magazine is used to communicate with both the employees and the franchisees. The magazine, very much like the corporate Web sites of international brands, covers company news, events and top sales rewards with trips overseas.

Continuing Education

In 1999, five years after the company was established, Liang Zi wanted to improve her knowledge of fashion design. She chose a three-month program of modelling at the Chambre Syndicale De La Couture Paris, long known as a place of fashion

Figure 3.2 Clothes made in Shu Liang. Photographer: Yu Jian.

Figure 3.3 Clothes made in Shu Liang. Photographer: Yu Jian.

pilgrimage. However, because she was married and had just had a baby, she hesitated to make the trip to the Paris school. For one thing, as the sole creator of the brand, she was irreplaceable.

Her husband finally pushed her to make the journey. He believed that designers need to constantly update their knowledge and international mindset. In 2001, Liang Zi again attended an overseas seminar, this time a six-month program of fashion design at the Fashion Institute of Technology in New York.

While she was studying overseas, she sketched designs, then faxed them back to the office to have her assistant monitor the production. Managing the company long-distance was 'certainly not satisfying, and could not compare with when I am managing it myself', said Liang Zi. But looking back, she said, 'It was still worthwhile.'

Studying in Paris and New York totally changed her perception of design. Prior to the overseas training, she had felt insecure about her drawing skills, and worried that her designs would not be appreciated by the instructors. The advanced training taught her that what she lacked in fashion design was not skill, but self-confidence. 'I learned to relax when designing, and that is when a good design eventually flows out.'

Living in the international fashion capitals also allowed Liang Zi to learn the lifestyles of local people. 'Now I understand why Paris and New York are the world-class fashion capitals. If you understand the people's lifestyles over there, you will know why.' She has ambitions for breaking into the international market. 'But we are a long-way behind the international brands,' said Liang Zi. 'It will be a long journey.'

Huang Zhi-Hua: Husband and Business Partner

Like Liang Zi, Huang Zhi-Hua also came from a rural family. He worked as a mechanical labourer, a teacher in a primary school and a journalist for a local newspaper before he entered college. Hard living conditions in his childhood gave him a maturity that boys his age don't normally possess. While working for the Zhejiang Silk Importing & Exporting Group, he was promoted from a designer position to the head of a sub-factory in Shenzhen due to his outstanding performance. Nowadays he spends most of his energy managing the four Tangy factories. Liang Zi once commented that without Zhi-Hua, Tangy would not have achieved success.

DIALOGUE

'A brand with no embodiment of culture is like a flower made of plastic.'

'Chinese roots' was probably the term used most frequently by Liang Zi in interviews. Unlike most other fashion brands, whose designers started business by copying trendy styles from international magazines, Tangy

Figure 3.4 Liang Zi's show at China Fashion Week in 2003.
Photographer: Yu Jian.

Figure 3.5 Liang Zi's show at China Fashion Week in 2005.
Photographer: Yu Jian.

Figure 3.6 Liang Zi's show at China Fashion Week in 2005.
Photographer: Yu Jian.

Figure 3.7 Liang Zi's show at China Fashion Week in 2005.
Photographer: Yu Jian.

区志航 摄

Figure 3.8 Liang Zi's show at China Fashion Week in 2006.
Photographer: Ou Zhi-Hang.

Figure 3.9 Catalogue shooting of 2006 Spring/Summer line.
Photographer: Juan Zi.

Figure 3.10 Catalogue shooting of 2006 Spring/Summer line.
Photographer: Juan Zi.

Figure 3.11 Catalogue shooting of 2006 Spring/Summer line.
Photographer: Juan Zi.

Figure 3.12 Catalogue shooting of 2008 Spring/Summer line.
Photographer: Juan Zi.

Figure 3.13 Catalogue shooting of 2008 Spring/Summer line.
Photographer: Juan Zi.

Figure 3.14 Catalogue shooting of 2008 Spring/Summer line.
Photographer: Juan Zi.

Figure 3.15 Catalogue shooting of 2008 Spring/Summer line.
Photographer: Juan Zi.

Figure 3.16 Catalogue shooting of 2009 Spring/Summer line.
Photographer: Juan Zi.

Figure 3.17 Catalogue shooting of 2009 Spring/Summer line.
Photographer: Juan Zi.

Figure 3.18 Liang Zi's show at China Fashion Week in 2008.
Photographer: Yu Jian.

Figure 3.19 Liang Zi's show at China Fashion Week in 2008.
Photographer: Yu Jian.

Liang Zi and Huang wanted their brand to be a reflection of Chinese culture. As such, they got the inspirations for the brand through reading and travelling. 'We do not just directly adopt the tradition. What we do is to use the traditions as media, then translate them into international language.' In Tangy's collection, one rarely sees the ubiquitous *Qi Pao* dress, which is often regarded as the traditional costume of the Chinese.

From where do you get inspirations for your collection every season?

I travel a lot. Normally, before the start of each season, I go somewhere that may be inspirational to me. I just came back from Li Jiang [a small town in Yun Nan Province, where many minority tribes dwell] because I heard they still sustain a sort of old technique in making *Yun Jing* [a type of old Chinese brocade]. I will use this fabric for my next collection. In general I think life experience is the key for my inspiration. What I see, learn and experience every day eventually inspires my work.

What is your signature design?

Obviously *Shu Liang* now is my hallmark. Tangy now is connected with *Shu Liang* whenever people talk about it. In general, my design is simple, easy-to-wear fashion but intertwined with a Chinese spirit.

Do you have any Western designers that you admire?

There are a lot, but their names are too long to remember [Laughs...] you know I'm still trying to improve my English.

As a fashion designer, what are the main challenges for you today? How did they differ from the challenges at the start-up phase?

Our main challenges today are the Chinese lifestyle and the credibility issue. Normally, Chinese people like to spend their leisure time at the Mahjong table. The lifestyle decides how much attention you give to your attire. I like spending my spare time in out-door sports. It relieves stress and provides inspiration. Credibility is another prevailing issue today. I have been hoodwinked by friends several times. I think it is stupid to lie to people, because no one will trust you a second time. But still lots of cheating and lying go around. It is a shame.

When we just started the business, of course money was a big issue. Fortunately we eventually made a profit. Now we have the money, but we find it difficult to find young talent. Young designers have very little knowledge about the technical facet of making clothes. They only know flat drawing on a piece of paper. But you know it is not all about design.

MA KE: A DESIGNER LIVING HER OWN VALUES

Ma Ke's private label, Exception, established in 1996, is widely regarded as the icon of the Chinese contemporary designer brands in China. Exception is considered as a contemporary designer brand because it was the first Chinese fashion brand featuring an obvious designer's temperament rather than having a typical 'Chinese' flavour. It is successful because its annual revenue is more than 100 million RMB, a level deemed the pinnacle in designer brands.

PORTFOLIO

Born: in the city of Changchun, Jilin Province, in 1971. Now based in the city of Zhuhai, Guangdong Province.

Education: obtained associate bachelor's degree in Fashion Design and Fashion Model Performance from the Suzhou Institute of Silk Science, 1992.

Career: Designer, Guangdong Hui Long Co., 1993; Design Director, Hong Kong Jin Long Group, 1995; established the brand Exception with her husband, 1996.

Selected Awards

1994, Golden Award, Brother Cup China International Young Designers Contest
1998, Best Design of the Year Award and Best Quality of the Year Award by CHIC
2004, Womenswear Brand of the Mode Award, China Fashion Week
2007, *Elle* Style Awards

Selected Public Commendations

We were told that Ma Ke would be the most difficult one to interview of all the planned-to-interview designers this time because she disliked doing interviews. Fortunately our editor had met her husband one time, otherwise it might have been even more difficult to get in contact with her. Although she finally agreed to do an interview, Ma Ke still refused to have her photo taken afterwards. (Wu 2006: 152)

Ten years ago, the then-twenty-five-year-old Ma Ke was chosen to be one of the 'Top Ten Fashion Designers'. She won first place in the Brother Cup design contest—the equivalent of an Oscar Award in the fashion regime at the time. She established the first brand truly featuring a designer temperament in China with Exception. In just ten years, Exception has become one of the best-known clothing brands [in China], but its design director Ma Ke has been keeping a low-key profile, hardly to be seen in the public and in the media. Ten years later, Ma Ke started a new journey by presenting her new brand, Useless, at Paris Fashion Week. (Xiao 2007)

Selected International Exposure

1999, paraded at the China Cultural Week in Paris
2007, paraded at Paris Fashion Week, 2007 Fall / Winter Collection
2008, presented at the exhibition of 'China Design Now' in the Victoria and Albert Museum in London

BIOGRAPHY
A Girl's Dreams (Prior to 1989)

When she was still a little girl, Ma Ke's first dream was to be a biologist like a woman scientist she'd heard about who was spending all her life in a primeval African forest studying orangutans. She later found another interest: art. She was fascinated with pictures and paintings in books, and did quite well copying them. But her father was a philosophy professor and he strongly opposed her desire to follow art. In the 1970s through the 1980s, Chinese parents as well as schools believed that only science and engineering would earn an individual three square meals; art was not going to bring in the bread. But little Ma Ke was so invested in her art that she just could not stop painting. She even learned to sketch on paper while pretending to listen to the teacher.

Her parents failed in their attempts to stop their daughter from continuing her dream of being an artist. One year before university entrance exams, her mother finally registered her in a three-month intensive fine arts program.

To be admitted to the professional fine arts school was beyond Ma Ke's wildest dreams, since she was only an amateur. So she switched to programs that were related to art. She had seen her mother sew clothes since she was a little girl, and the fascinating, beautiful clothes of her childhood made her choose the Fashion Design and Fashion Model Performance program.

Days in School (1989–1992)

Not understanding the difference between the Fashion Design and Fashion Model Performance program and the Fashion Design program, she chose the one with the longer name. The longer-name program covered both design and modelling while fashion design only had the one focus. When she inquired about the difference at the school, she was given the same explanation—that graduates from the Fashion

Design and Fashion Modelling program could be either a model or a designer. It was open to those interested in both subjects and fitting the physical size requirements.

The class proved to be a mix of the two programs—fashion modelling and fashion design. However, the course made the students strong neither in model performance nor design. In hindsight, Ma Ke felt the course spent too much time on social entertainment. The students frequently participated in all kinds of entertainment shows in hotels and restaurants, because their fees were much lower than that of the professional models. Not until the last year of school did Ma Ke decide to alter her focus. The modelling circle seemed too shallow and materialistic to her, so she switched to the department of Fashion Design. Despite diligent study in that last year, by the time she graduated she still knew very little about design.

With the Hong Kong Company (1993–1995)

By coincidence, after she left school, Ma Ke found a job in Guangzhou with a small clothing importing and exporting firm. She expected to be its designer, but in fact ended up helping her boss sell clothes. She later joined a Hong Kong fashion company where she learned the concept of branding for the first time.

Working for a Hong Kong company in the 1990s was regarded as prestigious in China, because it generally meant a high income, comfortable working environment and a high degree of professionalism. For Ma Ke it meant her first chance to practice designing in real life.

In 1994, Ma Ke proposed to enter her work, 'Qin Soldier', in the Brother Cup contest. The inspiration for her work came from the famous ancient monument of soldiers left by the first Chinese Emperor, Qin Shi-Huang. Her expectations were modest: 'Not to be the worst one'. She did not know if she qualified as a designer, but far beyond her expectation, she won first place. The win brought her to the attention of an interested Italian journalist who offered her the opportunity to study in Italy. Ma Ke refused the kind invitation. Like many other Chinese designers, Ma Ke believed that the place where one was born and where one lived provided design inspiration. All she had wanted from the contest was confirmation that she was a good designer, and her win settled the matter.

Winning the contest also brought her fame in the industry. The following year she was named one of the Top Ten Chinese Fashion Designers. Newly confident after winning the Brother Cup contest, she proposed that her employer launch a new brand designed for the young, trendy modern Chinese women.

In order to convince her manager, Ma Ke conducted intensive research and made a comprehensive proposal for the new brand. She eventually gained consent from the manager. In 1996, she presented her debut collection in Beijing, representing the new brand she created for the Hong Kong firm. Despite her lack of experience in directing fashion shows, Ma Ke earned applause after the show. Her manager finally decided to invest in the new brand.

Unfortunately, a harsh economic reversal followed. The company's main income came from exporting, but its business was severely debilitated by the trade barriers imposed by the United States and Europe in the mid 1990s. The company had to lay off most of its laborers, and abolish plans for the new brand. Ma Ke's once-glittering dream was shattered.

Starting Her Own Business with the Brand Exception (1996–)

Deeply frustrated, Ma Ke quit and went back home. A few large clothing companies approached her, offering millions of RMB in remuneration, including a house and car, but Ma Ke turned down all of them. Material things were not what Ma Ke valued the most. She was looking for someone who truly appreciated the value of design to the brand. But what the companies desired was Ma Ke's fame, not her design talent.

Her daily life was back to the way it was when she attended school—reading, thinking and dreaming. Ma Ke felt like she was losing her way again. Then one day when she was taking a mid-day nap, a whim seized her: why not start a business of her own? She called her husband, and to her surprise, his reaction was swift and positive. He then convinced one of his best friends to invest in the business.

The plan was soon placed into action and the Exception line was born. The friend invested 200,000 RMB for the company in late 1996. In actuality, it was a 'working studio' rather than a company, because Ma Ke was the only staff member. Her husband was still working for another company at the time. Ma Ke had to do everything herself, from sourcing, designing and making the clothes to searching the selling channels. Like many new ventures, starting out was arduous. The initial hardship undermined the investor's faith and he requested the return of his investment.

After a spirited discussion, Ma Ke and her husband decided to carry on with the venture. They made an agreement with the friend that the remainder of the investment would be turned into a loan, so that the business could continue.

After the first collection came out, Ma Ke asked two of her best friends to sell her line. One opened a boutique solely for Ma Ke's line, and the other sold Ma Ke's line in her existing shop. The sales were surprisingly good.

Not long after, however, Ma Ke visited one of the shops and found the Exception labels on her products had been replaced by a new name. Even more astonishing was that the new label belonged to the shop owner—the best friend. This friend had substituted her own label because she aimed to become the owner of the line once she realized sales were soaring. The best friend had even bought the other shop without telling Ma Ke.

This betrayal was another setback for Ma Ke. She had lost not only a close friend but also the just-built selling channels. Ma Ke decided she would rather lose the stores than continue business with her former friend, even though the friend believed no other stores would sell a new young designer's line. The heavy debt, the loss of the friendship, together with the close of the stores, forced Ma Ke once again to re-evaluate the development of her brand.

At this crucial point, her husband provided full and firm support to Ma Ke. He quit his job and joined Ma Ke's business. The couple decided to open and run their own stores directly. Sales ceased for two months before they spotted a superior location. It was an ideal place for selling the designer's line, but it was also very expensive. The amount of capital left from the original investor was only enough to operate the company for four months. If the shop failed to generate enough sales volume within four months, they would go bankrupt.

Ma Ke was faced with another turning point in her life, one that would decide her destiny as a designer. Guided by her instinct, Ma Ke rented the space. When the money was paid to the landlord, she felt like she was gambling away her life.

Fortune once again smiled on Ma Ke. Sales soared after the line launched in the new shop. In the first year the couple still paid close attention to each penny they had in the bank, but not at the expense of sacrificing design or quality of product. One year later, they cleared their debt with the former investor.

Unlike most business owners, the couple was not anxious to expand the brand swiftly. With the lessons already learned, they preferred sustainability and growth at a controlled pace. The brand of Exception and Ma Ke gradually became recognized names in fashion circles as well as the market. The designer gained a group of loyal fans very much like herself: young, well-educated, independent, intelligent and looking for uniqueness in clothing—a typical, modern Chinese young lady.

The following story gives a vivid depiction of the popularity of the brand in the market. In 2003, piracy of the design of Exception was prevalent in the market. The pirates usually went to the store and bought the top-selling styles, copied the pattern and material, then returned the products to the store, saying they were the wrong size or defective in quality. Ma Ke found her styles were being sold in other shops, but under different labels. Her sales clerks reported that the buyers were always the same group of people and they showed up frequently. The market share was severely affected by the illegal copies, since the pirates offered their copies at a lower price. As a consequence, Ma Ke closed all her stores in Shenzhen by 2003 and focused her sales in other cities.

Now Exception is the leading designer brand in China.

New Line: Useless (2006–)

In February 2007, Ma Ke was invited to present at the Haute Couture Show of Paris Fashion Week. Instead of presenting her mature line of Exception, she created a new line labeled 'Useless'. The Useless line was made of hand-woven natural-fiber fabrics, in order to promote the concept of ecology. Emanating a primitive and austere aura, the line mirrors the values and philosophy held by the designer herself. It is a line more suitable for museum exhibition and artistic display than the commercial market.

Because the Useless line was largely exempted from the push for sales revenue, the pressure on Ma Ke's design talents was relaxed—the dream of most designers. Ma Ke manifested her ability in designing through this artistic line. The line was later exhibited in the prestigious Victoria and Albert Museum in London.

DIALOGUE

What does design mean to you?

Design to me is about expressing myself from my heart. Exception was initially designed for me to wear. Lucky me, I found a group of people who shared my same values.

Where do you normally get your inspiration for your design?

Most of my design works were inspired by experiencing new things or exploring new material. I like to try different materials that nobody has ever used before. I'm not the type of person who cares so much about numbers, criticism, marketing... I never go to see my stores, never read any trendy magazines, I don't even know who's wearing my clothes, I design what I think fits me.

Who is your idol?
Martin Margiela and Rei Kawakubo.

How do you recruit a designer?
I judge firstly based on her or his values, secondly their passion for fashion.

What is your major challenge as a designer today?
Deny myself, then keep progressing.

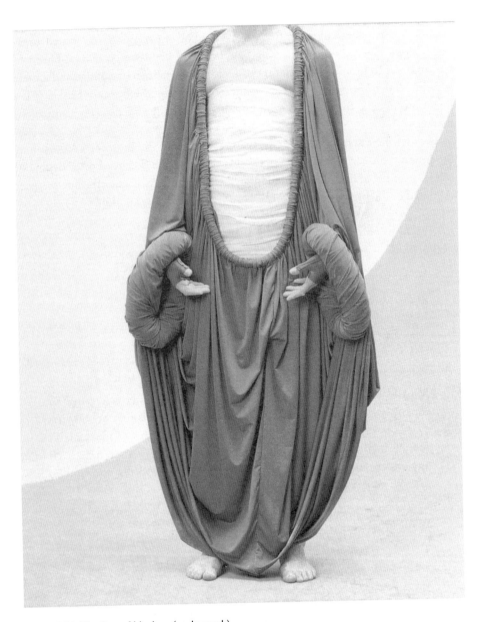

Figure 3.20 The line of Useless (early work).
Photographer: Wang Wen-Liang.

Figure 3.21 The line of Useless (early work).
Photographer: Wang Wen-Liang.

Figure 3.22 The line of Useless (early work).
Photographer: Wang Wen-Liang.

Figure 3.23 The line of Useless (early work).
Photographer: Wang Wen-Liang.

Why did you not use your own name as the name of the brand, just like most of the other designers have done?

A brand is the result of teamwork. My name was given to me by my parents. It is a personal asset. The lifecycle of a brand is supposed to be longer than that of a person. When I die someday, the brand needs to be carried on by somebody else. I am just a founder. Using my name for a brand's name is just not fair to others contributing to the brand. Brand has spirit, soul and values. It is like an independent person. I'm not interested in being a celebrity, but the brand should be a star.

Figure 3.24 The line of Useless (early work).
Photographer: Wang Wen-Liang.

Do you regard yourself as a successful designer?

I don't like the word *successful*. Everyone has a different definition for success. Maybe you think it successful but I don't think so. I think the most important thing is to be loyal to your own heart—do what you like to do, and make your own life valuable to others.

Please comment on your husband. Many people think you are lucky to have your husband as your business partner.

I am lucky that I don't need to worry about the marketing things by myself. He is quite supportive of my work, although we also argue with each other

Figure 3.25 The line of Useless (early work).
Photographer: Wang Wen-Liang.

sometimes. I am quite a persistent person, so he is very generous with me. He certainly deserves my thanks.

In 2006, Ma Ke created an artistic clothing line called *Wuyong*, meaning 'Useless' in English. Wuyong aims to discover the values of those seemingly useless objects, or create something that may be useless for the time being but useful in the future. In

Figure 3.26 The line of Useless (early work).
Photographer: Wang Wen-Liang.

Ma Ke's view, values of objects keep varying as time goes on. Something we regard useful for the time being eventually may be proved to be useless. Something we think useless now may turn out to be useful in the future.

The following interview was conducted through e-mail in the summer of 2009 after the launch of Useless in Paris.

Compared to our last interview [*note: which was done more than three years ago*], I noticed you had changed your outlook a lot. In our last interview, your responses were still quite 'ego-centric', but now you care more about the future of community, society and mankind. Obviously Wuyong is a

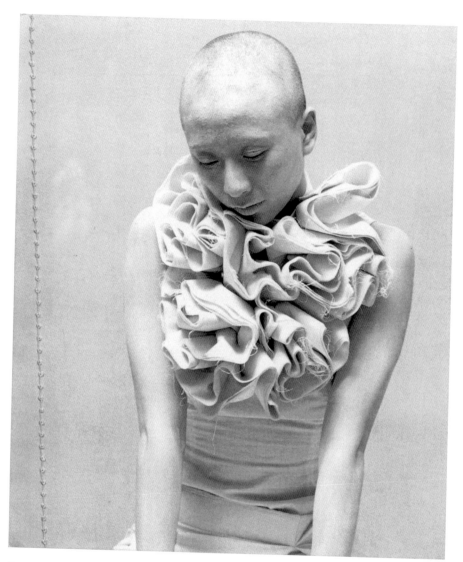

Figure 3.27 The line of Useless (early work).
Photographer: Wang Wen-Liang.

vehicle that conveys your values about life other than just a piece of clothing to wear. What do you feel are the most important personal changes
you've made in the past few years?

The 'self' idea is probably the most difficult hurdle that prevents one from
improving oneself. My next goal is 'no self'. I chose to follow my heart
as I grew up, but I also remind myself not to judge the world just by my

Figure 3.28 The line of Useless (early work).
Photographer: Wang Wen-Liang.

personal knowledge. Tolerance gives us a broader vision. If one wants to extend himself and eliminate tunnel vision, he must learn to be tolerant and observe the world from a different perspective. Now I understand there are many things in this world that are neither wrong nor right, and we don't always need answers for everything.

What made you change? I know you are a person who likes to explore new ideas and thinking. But is there any specific reason behind all the changes?

I think it is my age and life experience. Every time when I started my new journey, especially when I was far away from the urban life and in

Figure 3.29 The line of Useless presented in Paris 2008.
Photographer: Zhou Mi.

Figure 3.30 The line of Useless presented in Paris 2008.
Photographer: Zhou Mi.

Figure 3.31 The line of Useless presented in Paris 2008.
Photographer: Zhou Mi.

Figure 3.32 The line of Useless presented in Paris 2008.
Photographer: Zhou Mi.

Figure 3.33 The line of Useless presented in Paris 2008.
Photographer: Zhou Mi.

Figure 3.34 The line of Useless presented in Paris 2008.
Photographer: Zhou Mi.

the remote countryside, the majestic grand snowy mountain and the vast luscious landscape, which were there centuries ago, it evoked a memory of our ancestors' philosophy. I found no matter how developed the technology and economy is today, what we desire and cherish from the bottom of our hearts have never changed. So what are the values of all the new developments? I think mankind is in a bad place: what we are pursuing today brings us pain and despair. From this perspective I think the ideology of *Wu Wei*[4] created by our ancestors is full of wisdom.

What was the background of the birth of Wuyong? Is it a result of passion for creation, or just for the exhibition in Paris?

I decided to create a line solely from the heart and this was how the Wuyong line was born. But at day's end, is not all artwork created for life? I think there is nothing more important than creating your own life's journey. Exhibitions and shows only last for a moment. What we must accomplish in life is how we spend our every single day.

Figure 3.35 The line of Useless (2007).
Photographer: Zhou Mi.

Figure 3.36 The line of Useless (2007).
Photographer: Zhou Mi.

Have you considered what you will do if the Wuyong line is not as commercially successful as the Exception line? Or let's put it in this way, before you have the bread, will you still have opportunity to create this
artistic line?

Luckily I had not worked for bread before I had the bread. The birth of
Exception was just like Useless—it came from the heart. Its success is a

Figure 3.37 The line of Useless (2007).
Photographer: Zhou Mi.

Figure 3.38 The line of Useless (2007).
Photographer: Zhou Mi.

Figure 3.39 The line of Useless (2007).
Photographer: Zhou Mi.

bonus, but it was not my original goal. Struggling for survival is natural. The difference is what you choose to do after you learn how to survive. The fact is most people are struggling because of their endless greed, not just struggling to survive. Only a small number of people choose the harshest journey as they pursue their beliefs. They can abandon everything, even the bread, just to hold firmly to their beliefs. We need bread to support our physical body in order to realize what we believe in, but bread alone cannot sustain us.

The pictures of the Useless line are amazing. Do you tend to make Useless solely an artistic work, or will you eventually extend it to a commercial commodity? As the designer of Useless, do you regard yourself as a clothing designer, meaning clothing is a result in this context, or an artistic designer, meaning clothing is just a form used to express your artistic spirit?

Nowadays artwork trades like commodity anyway, otherwise how can such an abundance of businessmen earn their bread? To me the essential difference between artwork and commodity does not lie in trading—both of them are the *results* of creation and as such, both of them can be traded. The difference is the *reasons* why they are created—meaning their origination. Those created for faith and joy are art; for fame and benefits are commodity. I define success as *not* creating for selling and fame. Let people decide if Useless should be extended to a commercial line. If people like it, I would love to share my values through Useless.

Figure 3.40 The line of Useless (2007).
Photographer: Zhou Mi.

As the chief designer for both Exception and Useless, what are the positions of the two lines in your mind?

I'm the art director of Exception now. I hired a group of young designers and guide and support them to accomplish the design work. The line Useless was created for my retirement project, meaning it is something I can play with when I retire. Lucky me that I retired when I was just thirty-five years old!

How is Exception performing now? Are there any changes in its design style?

It is stable and growing. The design style has some changes due to the involvement of the younger designers. But the spirit of the brand remains the same.

WANG YI-YANG: SIMPLICITY AND AUSTERITY

BRIEF

Of all the interviewees, Wang Yi-Yang was the shyest. He preferred to be interviewed through e-mail rather than face-to-face, but agreed to this interview. When asked questions, he usually waited a few seconds, then slowly talked word by word.

Yi-Yang may not be as well known as the other interviewees in China, for he is a very low-key person. In the interviews, he spent most of the time talking about design rather than his personal life.

Yi-Yang was chosen for this list because he was the first chief designer of the once-cult-like modern Chinese fashion brand Layefe, and his two brands—Zuczug and Cha Gang—are widely acknowledged by industry professionals as well as in the market.

PORTFOLIO

Born: in 1971 in Changchun, Liao Ning Province. Now he lives in Shanghai.

Education: bachelor's degree in Fashion Design from the Dong Hua University, 1992.

Career: Lecturer in Dong Hua University, 1993–1996; Chief Designer of local fashion label Layefe, 1997–2001; established Zuczug and Cha Gang with a business partner, 2002.

Selected Award

1994, Bronze Prize award, Brother Cup International Fashion Design Contest

Selected Public Commendation

Cha Gang, as a high-end brand, is made in small quantities but delicately. It is trying to explore fashion from our daily life. (Sina.com: 2005)

Selected International Exposure

2008, China Design Exhibition, in Victoria and Albert Museum in London

Brands: Zuczug and Cha Gang

Zuczug was established in 2002, targeting contemporary young Chinese women with mid to high income. Its irregular form and size is best suited for tall, slim women. Only plain, natural colours are used for this line.

Cha Gang is a unique brand with its own mystique. *Cha* means 'tea' in Chinese, *Gang* means 'mug'. To Chinese people born in the 1960s through the 1970s Cha Gang had a very special meaning. It was one of the most popular daily articles used by Chinese families until the late 1980s. Back then, everyone—especially men—had two mugs: one for the office, and one for home. The mugs were white with a blue rim. The Cha Gang held a larger amount of water than normal cups. It was also lightweight and easy to clean. To most people Yi-Yang's age, Cha Gang epitomizes their childhood, the austere but simpler and friendlier life.

As a designer brand sold in department stores, Zuczug encounters volume pressure from the stores too, so the designer has to compromise to a certain degree to meet market demands. But Cha Gang presents more of the original values of the designer. The clothes, in a plain colour, are mostly inspired by old men and women wearing a blue or white muslin vest or T-shirt, sitting or lying on their bamboo chairs outside their homes and enjoying the sunshine in the lane, solitary but peaceful.

BIOGRAPHY

Yi-Yang's clothes mirror his personality: implicit, gentle, simple and austere, but with lavish nuance.

Unlike most of the other interviewed designers who experienced many ups and downs in their lives, Yi-Yang's life seems more pedestrian by comparison. Yi-Yang chose to study fashion design because of his fascination with painting. But his painting skills were not good enough to get into the top fine arts school, so the fashion drawing course neatly fulfilled his desire to be an artist.

Yi-Yang chose teaching at the university after he graduated. This is quite common for graduates who like a stable and simple life. Only students of distinction have the privilege of working for the colleges.

In 1997, Yi-Yang's destiny was changed by a man named Chen Yi-Fei. Chen Yi-Fei was one of the most celebrated painters in China in 1997. He completed his fundamental studies in painting in China, and then went to New York for further education. He became a prominent artist after his work started being collected by New York mainstream galleries and museums. Some of his paintings still hold the record for highest auction price paid for works by a contemporary Chinese artist. Chen Yi-Fei died of disease in 2005.

Chen Yi-Fei built the fashion label Layefe in the late 1990s, in order to provide beautiful and affordable clothing for Chinese women. The Western brands provided beautiful clothes, but they were too expensive for most Chinese people. The local brands were cheap, but dull. Yi-Fei expected Layefe to fill the market gap.

To this day Yi-Yang does not know why Yi-Fei chose him as the designer for the new label. But he still remembers his enjoyable conversations with the celebrity. They shared the same values, and the artist let Yi-Yang be daring and innovative. Neither Chen nor Yi-Yang knew much about the mysteries of commercial brand building, but this probably contributed to the reason why Yi-Yang enjoyed his time spent with the company. The famous artist was mostly engaged with his artistic events and had little time to spend on the new brand. This allowed ample opportunity for Yi-Yang to learn, experience and explore the mysteries of designing and branding. The result rewarded both his boss and Yi-Yang. The goods sold exceedingly well, partly due to the fame the artist enjoyed in his native country.

When the sales skyrocketed, the owner decided to go public in order to get enough financial support for the company's operation. Eventually, a chain-of-command organization replaced the small, studio-type team and the atmosphere in the office became more commercialized and political. Yi-Yang chose to leave, eventually starting a business of his own.

In 2002, he partnered with a friend, who also came from Layefe, and together they built the brand Zuczug. The plan was simple—with the experience gained from Layefe, they believed they would be successful.

DIALOGUE

You don't talk very much, even when answering questions. Is this your usual way when interviewed?

[Smiles shyly, waits a few seconds.] Yeah, it is my way... I normally don't do interviews. Or I do interviews through emails. The interviewers send me a list of questions and I answer in writing. I just want to do what I like to do, instead of being somebody famous. I accepted your interview because this is a book for the Western market. Since it will represent Chinese designers, I'm honoured to be involved.

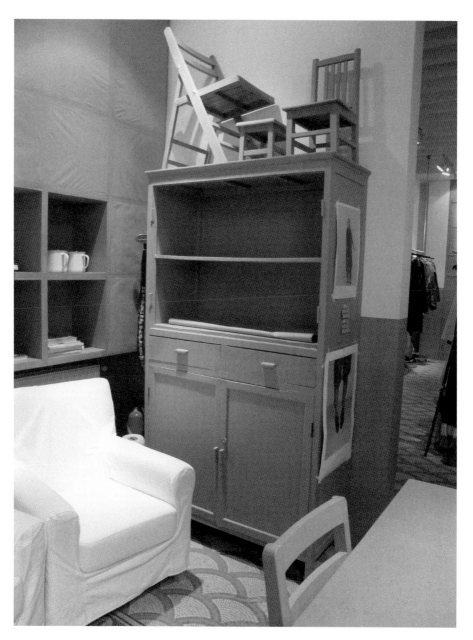

Figure 3.41 Cha Gang store. Photographer: Peng Yang-Jun.

Figure 3.42 Cha Gang store. Photographer: Peng Yang-Jun.

Figure 3.43 Cha Gang store. Photographer: Peng Yang-Jun.

Figure 3.44 Cha Gang store. Photographer: Peng Yang-Jun.

Figure 3.45 Image of Cha Gang (early work).
Photographer: Peng Yang-Jun.

Figure 3.46 Image of Cha Gang (early work).
Photographer: Peng Yang-Jun.

Figure 3.47 Image of Cha Gang (early work).
Photographer: Peng Yang-Jun.

Figure 3.48 Image of Cha Gang (early work).
Photographer: Peng Yang-Jun.

Figure 3.49 Image of Cha Gang (early work).
Photographer: Peng Yang-Jun.

Figure 3.50 Image of Cha Gang (early work).
Photographer: Peng Yang-Jun.

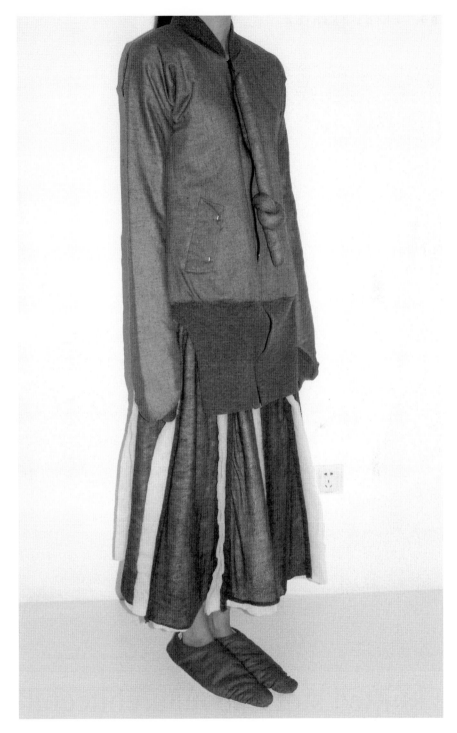

Figure 3.51 Image of Cha Gang (early work).
Photographer: Peng Yang-Jun.

a knitted story about architecture

Figure 3.52 Image of Cha Gang (latest work).
Photographer: Wang Yi-Yang.

a knitted story about architecture

Figure 3.53 Image of Cha Gang (latest work).
Photographer: Wang Yi-Yang.

a knitted story about architecture

Figure 3.54 Image of Cha Gang (latest work).
Photographer: Wang Yi-Yang.

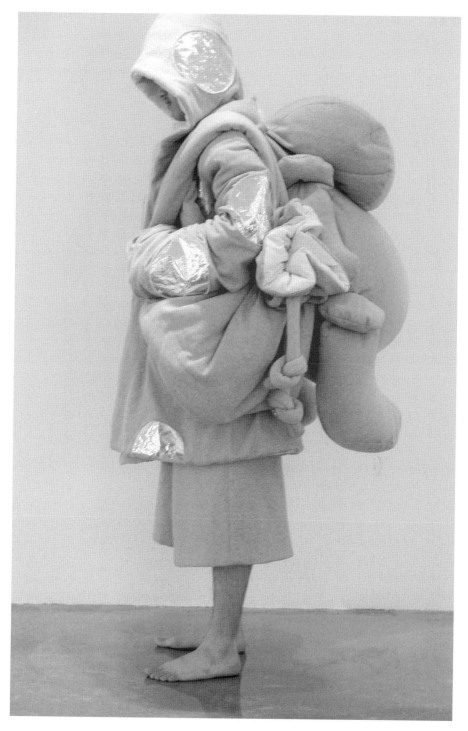

Figure 3.55 Image of Cha Gang (latest work).
Photographer: Wang Yi-Yang.

Figure 3.56 Image of Cha Gang (latest work).
Photographer: Wang Yi-Yang.

Figure 3.57 Image of Cha Gang (latest work).
Photographer: Wang Yi-Yang.

How do you spend your time usually?

I usually come to the office at 10:00 a.m. and leave at 11:00 p.m. I spend most of my time with fabric, sketches and designs, like most other designers. My life is quite simple. I don't have much of a night life. I do read if I am not designing.

Many designers feel confused by the roles of designers or artists. What do you think of the difference between a designer and an artist?

I think the line between designers and artists is less distinct today. More artists engage themselves in design works, and more designers show their work in art exhibitions. The crossover is quite prevalent now. Art to me is more spiritual, it reflects a person's values and thinking. Design is to transform the spirit to daily life. An artist is a theorist, and a designer is an engineer. An artist can work independently and freely, but a designer needs teamwork and good communication skills.

Many Chinese designers believe that to get into the international market it is important to be 'Chinese', so they adopt many Chinese elements in their design. What do you think of these Chinese elements?

How can one piece of design work cover the cultural history of a nation? A few elements do not represent all of the national culture. Because we showed too many *Qi Pao,* dragons, the Cultural Revolution and the image of red lanterns on clothing or films, it misled Westerners into thinking that these were all about 'Chinese'. I think it is important, as a designer, to show yourself honestly. There are more than these so-called Chinese elements in our daily lives. And I think it a good resource for the design. There is no need to highlight that we are Chinese designers. In the international market, I don't think people really care about where you are from. No one will give you more or less respect just because you are from a specific country. I think the more important thing is that your design fits your target group of people.

What do you think of the prospect of Chinese designers stepping into the mainstream of Western countries?

I think as a designer the most important thing is to truly know yourself, then express yourself honestly, regardless of where you are from. In an international market, wherever you are from—China, India or any other developing countries—you compete with your product, not where you are from. Many local designers complained about the working environment in China, such as the hard sourcing of good fabrics, no talent, tough department stores...but I think it is the same here as it is in other countries. In fact, I think now as Chinese designers we probably have more advantages than those in other countries, because we are in the largest market in the world, and our status is accelerating quickly. The big problem with local designers is they want to find a shortcut to achieve fame and success. This will not breed good designers.

Have you had a chance to communicate with Western designers and exchange ideas?

I was once invited to The Netherlands with a few other Chinese designers for an exhibition. I found them very open and free-minded. It reflects their culture of independence and equality. Compared to them, I think we looked less confident. Maybe in our mind we sort of believe they are stronger in the realm of arts than we are anyway. Actually I later found we should not feel inferior to them. They were very polite, and showed the same respect to us as they did others. They also spoke highly of our works. In terms of design methodology, I think we give more attention to the final result: how it looks, who will wear or use it. But they care more about the processing. I mean, the work is a result of a logical thinking and processing. It is not a result made for the result.

THE SECOND GENERATION OF CHINESE DESIGNERS: PROFESSIONALIZED, COMMERCIALIZED AND DIVERSIFIED

These three interviewed designers epitomize the development of the second generation of Chinese fashion designers. They mostly were born in the late 1960s and 1970s, achieved fame through all types of contests, experienced some setbacks in their lives and careers, then established businesses of their own from the mid 1990s to the beginning of the twenty-first century. They are the mainstay of the designer brands in China today!

Compared to the first generation, they are very fortunate because they grew up in a period of crucial transition in China.

By the mid 1990s, Chinese people had broadened views and a more open and free mindset. Clothes were no longer political statements. The majority of people still had a blind fascination for the international brands, but a new kind of Chinese woman was emerging: she either worked in foreigner-invested companies or had her own business, travelled around the world, had good taste in fashion and wanted clothes with personality.

The freer economic infrastructure attracted many investors from the Western countries, Hong Kong and Taiwan. It is worth noting that the quick expansion of Chinese fashion labels is largely attributable to the Hong Kong and Taiwan investors. As the first group of investors from different markets, they not only raised the income bar for local labourers, but also brought new concepts, management skills and marketing tactics to Chinese managers, especially in the field of branding and retailing.

Private business was another booming force that influenced the development of the Chinese economy. Unlike the first generation of entrepreneurs, this generation received good educations, were open-minded, gained valuable experience from the state-owned companies and the foreigner-invested companies and eventually explored a formula of their own to build successful business in the Chinese market.

The clothing industry is becoming more pragmatic and skilful in promoting designers. But compared with the designer brands, the clothing administration institutions and the education academies still remained stagnant in the 1990s. Some progress was made in the institutional and educational units, for instance inviting more international professionals to join the contest judges' panels, adopting the education system used overseas and sending more teachers overseas to study. One good result is the establishment of the Raffles Design Institute through an interactive partnership with overseas institutions. Although it is not the top-ranked design school internationally, the Raffles Design Institute provides a fresh methodology in teaching the design course. It requires no entrance exams as long as the expensive tuition is met. Most of its lecturers are either from Singapore (it's a Singapore-based college) or Western countries. The design course covers a wider spectrum, from creating to drawing, cutting, making and marketing. So the students receive comprehensive training about the design process. In the course, drawing is not valued as the most important skill; instead creativity and the way to translate the concept to final clothes is where the emphasis is placed.

The majority of the private ventures in the clothing industry started out as mom-and-pop enterprises. The clothing industry was one of the earliest to privatize, and the mom-and-pop format is certainly a more stable business partnership. Such relationships provide a concrete foundation for the development of the business, hence creating a more sustainable brand.

Obviously, the designers of the second generation are more pragmatic and down-to-earth, learning from the experiences of the first generation—that designers' careers would be short-lived if they did not affiliate with concrete brands.

The designers born in the 1970s still carry the qualities of diligence, warmth and enthusiasm, because of the poor but affectionate typical Chinese family life they experienced in childhood. The traditional Chinese spirit was echoed by the designer artefacts, only in a different format.

Compared to the straight Chinese look of the earlier generation, the younger breed translated the Chinese format to a more subdued, sometimes even imperceptible, outlook. But you still sense the 'Chinese' essence. The obvious Chinese icons such as *Qi Pao* or dragons are hardly seen in the new generation's work. What is mostly seen are the spiritual and philosophical facets—harmony, peace, quiet, natural— originating from traditional Chinese values. In addition, they were influenced by promising international contemporary designers such as those from Belgium and The Netherlands. This all gives a variety and diversity to the design styles, such as deconstructing the clothes through different cutting techniques, or exploring new materials for a fresh look.

The second generation is more pragmatic and professional, but not conservative. They care about media buzz and present shows occasionally, but these are not the be-all and end-all of their design lives. They do not tend to favour everyone's taste, but rather, look for the customers who echo their personal values. Once they find that group they are comfortable and relaxed with their design capability. This in turn allows more space for the design personality to shine, letting the designers express themselves from their hearts.

4 THE TWENTY-FIRST CENTURY: THE THIRD GENERATION—PROSPECTS

BACKGROUND
SOCIO-ECONOMIC CONDITIONS

As the twenty-first century began, China gradually became a central focus of the world's interest. The successful launch of a manned spaceship in 2003, later in 2005, and again in 2008; the hosting of the 2008 Olympic Games in Beijing; the average GDP growing at an annual rate of 9.8 per cent from 2001 through 2006; fiscal revenues increasing at 18 per cent; per capita disposable income of urban residents growing by 10 per cent—all increased China's visibility on the world stage. The overall quality of life in China—especially in the urban cities—has improved dramatically. Strong economic power stimulates consumption and changes lifestyles. Playing Mahjong is still very popular but mostly in lower-income families. Attending sports events, going to theatres and visiting art exhibitions are now in mode as well.

Culture-wise, more Chinese celebrities rocketed to international fame: actresses Gong Li and Zhang Zi-Yi, and athletes Yao Ming and Liu Xiang, to name a few.

Advances in technology make the world smaller than ever. Chinese young people see more international films, art exhibitions and other entertainment. Cities like Shanghai and Beijing host more international conferences and entertain more celebrities. Interactions are growing between China and the rest of the world. China's status in the world has increased, both politically and economically.

THE FASHION INDUSTRY

In the Chinese fashion industry, one obvious change in the new century is the increasing use of the word *international*. China Fashion Week changed its name officially to China International Fashion Week in 2000. Aimed at offering an international platform for Chinese designers, it promotes local designers on the catwalk and sends outstanding talent to the international fashion week. Shanghai launched the Shanghai International Fashion Federation in 2003. More international faces are seen at fashion events and various entertainments. When Chanel, Armani, Anna Sui, Marc Jacob all opened shops in China, the Chinese people realized that the names they once adored as 'big names' such as Montagut, Goldlion and Playboy were in fact unknown in the mainstream international market.

Another trend in the new century is that along with the growing economic power of Chinese clothing companies, more Western designers are coming to China to assume the positions of chief designers and/or designer directors in these companies. Smaller companies invite Western designers twice a year to coach local designers and give direction and critiques on the seasonal collections.

In addition, China International Fashion Week eliminated its title of 'festival' and its focus on entertainment, and is now more commercially oriented, thanks to lessons learned from overseas counterparts and past experiments. It reinforced its focus on the originality and creativity of designer brands in order to differentiate itself from other fashion weeks in China, which mostly focus on the trading of mass-market brands. It follows the business model of the international fashion weeks by engaging more celebrities, fashion models, fashion photographers and fashion journalists. The industry is in general more integrated. Catwalk shows are not only for entertainment purposes, but more for connecting with business collaborators, including department stores, journalists and the market.

To promote young design talent, cosmopolitan cities like Shanghai, Beijing and Shenzhen built free or inexpensive facilities called 'the Innovation Centre' for designers to create their works and sell their design pieces. The concept was borrowed from the 'Loft' idea of transforming old abandoned factories into trendy and innovative spaces. Just to name a few, there's 798 Artistic Centre in Beijing; the Tianzifang and the Moganshan Road, both in Shanghai; and the F518 Innovative Centre in Shenzhen.

Nowadays, Chinese department stores don't just chase after international brands, but they give more attention and space to local design brands as well.

The local clothing brands were segmented into a three-tiered pyramid by the new century. The local Chinese mass-market-brands represent the majority of the market share, and thus form the bottom part of the pyramid. Local Chinese designer-brands selling to people looking for personality and affordability form the second tier. Many of these second-tier designers also provide made-to-measure service to local celebrities and rich people. The top tier—meaning small volume but not necessarily top-ranked—consists of the youngest generation, mostly born in the 1980s, who chose to open boutiques right after graduating from college. One obvious change in this, the third generation, is that many of them went abroad to study design, then came back to open stores in China. Due to limited finances, they mostly opened boutiques with the limited funding support from the government (see aforementioned 'Innovative Centre'), or from their own savings and/or loans from families or friends. Normally they only owned one or two shops. The labels are not up to the level of branding yet, but they represent a new Chinese-look in fashion design.

Fashion Models

Although there have been several Chinese fashion models showing and casting for international brands, it is widely acknowledged that Du Juan was the first Chinese model to enter the leading international fashion brands mainstream when she paraded for Louis Vuitton in 2006.

Fashion Magazines

In 2001, *Harper's Bazaar* was imported to China through a partnership with the local magazine, *Fashion*.

In 2002, *Marie Claire* entered the Chinese market.

In 2005, *Vogue* landed in China.

Exposure Overseas

As one of the programs for the Sino–France Cultural Week in the Musee Louvre in October 2003, seven Chinese fashion designers presented shows.

Chinese designer Frankie Xie presented his brand Jefen in Paris Fashion Week on 1 October 2006. This was the first Chinese fashion brand paraded in the top four distinguished fashion weeks.

Ma Ke presented her brand Useless at the Haute Couture show of Paris Fashion Week in 2007.

An exhibition entitled 'China Design Now', hosted by the Victoria and Albert Museum in London, was on display from March through July 2008. The exhibition's aim was to promote the contemporary artefacts of young Chinese designers. Fashion designers Ma Ke, Wang Yi-Yang and Lu Kun were included.

Ji Wen-Bo, one of the most prominent men's wear designers in China, presented the brand Li Lang in Tokyo Fashion Week in September 2008.

Luo Zhen presented her brand of Omnialuo in New York Fashion Week in September 2008.

THE YOUNG TALENT DESIGNERS

Children born in the 1980s reached age twenty in the beginning of the twenty-first century. As the first generation born under the One-child Policy[1], these young people grew up in a fast-changing, quick-growing, more-open, energetic and interactive environment. Compared to their predecessors, they learn more quickly and are more actively engaged with the latest inventions. They are more confident and ego-centric.

Nowadays the tendency is for more Chinese students to study fashion design abroad due to the growing economic power of the Chinese people and easier access to fashion capitals like London, Paris, New York and Tokyo. The young overseas-trained students cannot be ignored. They are a visible force contributing to the emergence of the younger generation. Some local students started their own studios shortly after gaining work experience from large companies.

However, finding sufficient capital is still a big hurdle for young designers. Lack of experience and lack of a coaching system placed many of the young designers in a dilemma. Sometimes they even fought over plagiarism of each other's designs. On Changle Road—a young-designer boutique road in Shanghai—if one piece sells well, the same pieces will be seen in other boutiques nearby in a very short time. Due to funding issues, many young designers sometimes resort to copying another designer's pieces that sell well and then sell them in their own stores at a lower price in order to turn a faster profit.

These talented designers are too young to have much in the way of professional biographies, and no one has emerged from their midst as a spokesperson for their generation. Therefore, two young, promising designers, who have shown some talent, were selected to be interviewed because they epitomize the youngest generation.

LU KUN
PORTFOLIO

Born: in 1981 in Shanghai.

Education: Studied clothing design in the No. 2 Light Industry Polytechnical School in Shanghai in 2000.

Career: Worked as a pattern modifier in Replay Jeans (China) from 2001–2002; opened his own tailor's shop in 2002.

Selected Public Commendation

Don't always use the few top designers' names that everyone in the world would know to astonish [Chinese] people. In the large cosmopolitan city of Shanghai, there is a local designer called Lu Kun who amazed foreigners. (Man 2005: FOB)

Selected Public Shows

2004, debuted at the No. 3 on the Bund Road, Shanghai

2005, presented at the BMW Formula 1 Fashion Show, Shanghai

2005, presented in the Shangri-La Gala in London

2006, presented at the St. Regis Charity Night, Beijing

2006, presented at the Chinese and Russian Government Cultural Exchange, Moscow

2006, presented at Barranquilla Fashion Week, Barranquilla, Colombia

2007, presented at 2008 Spring/Summer New York Fashion Week, New York

2007, presented at the International Fashion Night Charity Show in Munich, Germany

2007, presented at the 2007 Fall/Winter Singapore Fashion Festival, Singapore

2008, exhibited at 'China Design Now' in the Victoria and Albert Museum, London

BIOGRAPHY

Looking at his resume, it is easy to believe him a fortunate young man. He debuted when he was younger than twenty-four, travelled to international fashion capitals—London, Moscow and Singapore—for big shows, received visits from top celebrities like Victoria Beckham, Paris Hilton, Vivian Tam, Jean Paul Gautier and Yue-Sai Kan.

Lu Kun is one of the rising stars of talented young designers born in the 1980s. Though he never attended any professional school, Lu Kun gained cutting skills by apprenticing with an old tailor and later enhancing his knowledge through a self-study program. Alexander McQueen is his idol. Very much like McQueen, Lu Kun was also born into a grass-roots family. His father is a worker in a landscape company, his mother is a housewife. Unlike most other designers who are ashamed of the term *tailor,* Lu Kun always calls himself a tailor.

Lu Kun's flair in cutting received high praise from international designers like Vivien Tam and Jean Paul Gautier, when they visited Shanghai in 2004 to present at the local fashion week, and from celebrities like Victoria Beckham, when she was invited to Shanghai as a special judge for the 2004 World Elite Model Pageant Final. Yue-Sai Kan, a legendary female entrepreneur and TV personality, also promoted Lu Kun's clothing in her talk show and invited Lu Kun to design clothes for some of her important public functions.

With no prominent educational background, and born into a poor family, but speaking good English and showing cutting and designing talent, Lu Kun attracted media attention by the interesting mix of his background. He loves the social life and likes to party. He provides beautiful clothing for free to local movie stars and

Figure 4.1 Lu Kun and Victoria Beckham.
Photographer: Liu Xun-Xuan.

fashion journalists, and anyone else he thinks important enough to promote his name.

Yet a great deal of public fame does not always help in generating revenue. Lu Kun's designs are fit only for slim and sexy women—a very small niche. The label costs 3,000–10,000 RMB per piece, close to that of a luxury label. Chinese women are not yet ready to pay for a local designer's piece that's as expensive as an international brand. This situation has forced Lu Kun to withdraw his lines from two top boutiques in Shanghai.

Lu Kun's dream is to build a genuine luxury brand. According to him, he has received inquiries from overseas investors but none of them had the courage to invest in his brand, because 'luxury brands are a high-risk venture.'

Figure 4.2 Lu Kun's design. Photographer: Vanh Wan.

Figure 4.3 Lu Kun's design. Photographer: Vanh Wan.

Lu Kun's studio now survives on income from two components: the made-to-measure service for clients, and the design service—mostly producing designs for uniforms for other brands. In the latest interview, Lu was working on a uniforms design project and feeling lost in his career because he did not know how exactly to achieve his goal of building a haute couture brand. The reasons, he says, are the harsh reality of zero funding and the immaturity of the local commercial system. 'I wanted to attend the *Project Runway*[2], but I'm not eligible because I'm not locally based. There are some international design programs that promote young design talents, but they require the candidates to have stores either in New York or London.'

For a while Lu Kun had a partner originally from Puerto Rico who grew up in the United States. With his Western background, the partner helped Lu Kun build connections overseas. He helped find sponsorships and got loans for Lu Kun's seasonal shows. Lu Kun's first live show was achieved through a loan of 200,000 RMB. He almost went bankrupt after the show, and had to work hard for several months in order to clear the debit. Unfortunately, the partnership broke up in 2007.

Figure 4.4 Sketch of Lu Kun's design. The Shanghai women
of the 1930s are a great inspirational source for his design.
Image courtesy of Lu Kun.

Figure 4.5 Sketch of Lu Kun's design. Image courtesy
of Lu Kun.

JI JI
PORTFOLIO

Born: in 1972 in Xin Jiang. Now based in Beijing and Shanghai.
Education: Obtained bachelor's degree in Industrial Products design from the Shanghai Jiao Tong University, 1994.

Figure 4.6 Ji Ji. Photographer: He Jing.

Career: Set up Poledesign consultancy firm in 1999. Prior to the establishment of his own business, Ji Ji worked in the marketing department for a toilet paper company for nearly six years.

Selected Public Commendations

Ji Ji is like the information centre containing all the profiles of the Shanghai young design talents, from street cultural magazine publishers to Web designers, from photographers to toy designers, from architects to musicians, he has the ability to gather the freshest, funniest, most vigorous designers around him. (Xie 2007)

Ji Ji, who was born in the 1970s, is an innovative Chinese designer. He adopts innovative and humorous, sometimes even ironic, language to transform the Chinese cultural symbols. (Shui 2008: B20)

Selected Public Shows

2005, presented at the Singapore Fashion Festival, Singapore
2006, presented at Berlin Fashion Week, Germany
2006, presented at the *Flower and Styling* China Young Fashion Design Talents show in Beijing
2008, exhibited at the 'China Design Now' show in the Victoria and Albert Museum in London

BIOGRAPHY

Though born in the early 1970s, Ji Ji is grouped in the youngest generation because he started to receive public buzz in 2005 after hosting several modern art exhibitions in Beijing and Shanghai, and later extending his design to the fashion business. He is included in this book because his studio is one of the few of the youngest generation that is profitable.

Ji Ji plays dual-roles in his company—businessman and chief designer. This gives him the acuteness of a businessman and the innovation of a designer.

Ji Ji studied industrial product design in college but worked in marketing for six years after graduation. 'A great learning process in my career', said Ji Ji. He attributed his achievements today to those six years working in the toilet paper company. 'Toilet paper is, you know, one of the products that are most difficult to promote, but we made it.' To Ji Ji, if you can successfully promote toilet paper, it is much easier to promote a fashion brand.

After leaving the toilet paper company, Ji Ji started a design service for a friend's company. He first started out doing graphic design and VI (Visual Identification) for businesses and eventually branched off into clothing design.

Ji Ji built a wide social network for himself through his design service for big brands like Nike, Adidas, Levi's and L'oreal. He is also close to models and young artists in the contemporary arts and pop music fields, a result of his organizing and hosting show events and exhibitions. Ji Ji cleverly consolidated his social network resources and used them for his brand building.

With support from friends he almost succeeded in getting funding of US$5 million from a professional investor in 2008. But the financial crisis ruined his dream.

Figure 4.7 Hipanda T-shirt. Hipanda is a high-street fashion brand targeting teenage boys and girls who favour pop music and arts and receive generous pocket money from their parents every month.

Figure 4.8 Hipanda T-shirt.

'It was like sitting in the Vertical Coaster', he said, referring to the wild roller coaster at Chimelong Paradise in China. He spent nearly US$30,000 on the business proposal to the investor, all for naught when the financial crisis swept the whole world.

But this financial reversal allowed time for Ji Ji to reconsider his business. The past few years he had been working on a tight schedule and he rarely had time to think about his future development. 'I had been busy with all kinds of events, shows and exhibitions in the past few years. I took a break in 2008 to do some deep thinking about my life and my career. What exactly I want to do, how I want to position myself. What is the difference of my clothing, how I should develop the brand...Now I'm clear again on my objectives.'

According to Ji Ji, he is still involved in the business side of branding, but in the long run he wants to fade out of the business end and focus more on design and arts.

Figure 4.9 Hipanda T-shirt.

THE THIRD GENERATION OF CHINESE DESIGNERS: THE GENERATION OF PROSPECTS?

Fortune favoured China at the turning point of the new century. More international brands have jumped into the Chinese market pool while local Chinese fashion brands are springing up. China is becoming an international market.

Compared to their predecessors, the younger breeds have broader views and a passion for style and innovation. The global atmosphere favours China and adds great value to the development of the generation. But, does this mean they will be successful in the near future?

There's no question that the young talents demonstrate design in a more contemporary, diversified and creative format. But looking deep down, the exceptional

Figure 4.10 Underoath line created by Ji Ji. Photographer: Ji Ji.

designers are people like Lu Kun, whose creations are original. Most of the younger designers still like copying others' works or imitating works from overseas designers. For instance, deconstruction is a prevailing design technique being used by many young designers nowadays in China. Contemporary young designers from England,

Figure 4.11 Underoath line created by Ji Ji.
Photographer: Ji Ji.

Figure 4.12 Underoath line created by Ji Ji. Photographer: Ji Ji.

Figure 4.13 Underoath line created by Ji Ji. Photographer: Ji Ji.

Figure 4.14 Underoath line created by Ji Ji. Photographer: Ji Ji.

Figure 4.15 Underoath line created by Ji Ji. Photographer: Ji Ji.

Belgium or The Netherlands are their idols. The difference is, when looking to those signature pieces of the international labels, you feel a philosophy and logic behind the clothes, whereas with the younger Chinese designers' works, very often what you feel is a superficial imitation. On Changle Road, the designer boutique street in Shanghai, a pair of young designers fought over the copying issue, and both parties said the design was their own. It may have been the original design of one of them, or it may have been a copy. We will never know. But many masters started out by imitating another master's work. Rather, the concerns should be that under the trend towards globalization, these young people—like so many young generations in other countries—are no longer fascinated by their country's history and national cultural relics. As globalization increases, there will probably be more similar-looking clothes in the shops and less iconic pieces.

Nevertheless, challenges remain. Statements like, 'As the largest world clothing manufacturing centre, China exports low priced/low quality clothes' have been imposed on most of the international market. How many international buyers will be convinced that Chinese designers' labels could sell well when they see labels that say 'Made in China'?

Funding is still an issue, worldwide. The industry needs more companies like LVMH, which launched the Young Artists Award to support up-and-coming young artists, and Ecco Domani, which supports the Ecco Domani Fashion Foundation to help young talents present their collections in New York Fashion Week. There are, in fact, quite a few Chinese enterprises and institutions that have burned through a lot of money for designers, though mostly for promoting their own names or political achievements. These enterprises generally make a one-time investment, host a show or exhibition for the designers, make noise in the media, then end the deal with the designers! The previously mentioned Innovation Centres are a good example. When a concept like the Innovation Centre is in vogue, everyone follows. This leads to an excessive number of Innovation Centres but few designers who will enjoy the benefits. For instance, one of the Lofts in Shanghai offers a very low rent to designers for studios and showrooms, but after a while many of the designers terminated their contracts with the Loft because neither buyers nor sales persons ever visited the space. These types of Loft projects are mostly for the city's image, an achievement in politics rather than essential support in commerce.

Lack of funding also prevents the younger generations from engaging in the top shows like China International Fashion Week. One of the criticisms given by spectators is that the primary eligibility factor to participate in the fashion week is money instead of talent.

Education certainly is a long-term challenge in China. The core principles and teaching methodology have not changed much over the years. There are, however, some exceptions in the top schools like the Beijing Fashion Institute and the China Academy of Arts and a few others. The overall education system in China has been criticized for some time because of its inflexible way of recruiting students, especially in the field of applied arts, and the overly academic backgrounds but little practical experience of its faculty.

Last but not least, both the country and the world are moving so fast that fewer investors have the patience to wait for businesses to grow. Consumers move their interest on to new styles in a shorter time, and trend lifecycles are getting shorter and shorter. Will young talents have the patience to hold to their faith firmly?

5 CONCLUSION

Since the revolution in China, the post-Mao era (1978–2008) has encompassed thirty years. Compared with the history of mankind, thirty years is the blink of an eye. But these past thirty years were an undeniable turning point in China's history.

Over the past three decades, this country of 1.3 billion in population has enjoyed an average annual GDP growth rate of 9 per cent. By 2006, the GDP in China was ranked number four world-wide.

Over the past three decades, the number of fashion institutions grew from a few to a few hundred; the number of fashion designers grew from a few hundred to more than a hundred thousand; the local fashion brands grew from a few to nearly a hundred thousand.

Over the past three decades, Chinese designer fashion brands evolved from copying Western labels to creating their own spirit of brand.

Over the past three decades, China has gradually moved her focus from 'making' to 'branding' and now 'creating'.

There is no question that this country with the largest population in the world is unique. One need only look at China's fast growth and dramatic evolution in general and her fashion industry in particular. I hope that after reading this book, you have a better understanding of the history of China and therefore the development of Chinese fashion designers. China is still a developing country and her designers are still far behind the international brands, but I hope the Chinese fashion designers will earn your respect.

Most of the first generation of designers hid their lights under a bushel, concentrating on teaching and coaching the younger generations. Some of them, like the ones listed in this book, still hold firmly to their dreams. I wish them luck. It has been nearly twenty years between the time the first Chinese fashion designer, Chen Shan-Hua, paraded in Paris in 1987, and Frankie Xie's Jefen brand showing in Paris Fashion Week on 1 October 2006. These designers have gone from being entertainers to genuine brand players, an achievement made by the generation as a whole rather than any single individuals. We should never forget they are the pioneers of the industry and paved the way for their followers. I salute the pioneers!

The second generation of designers are becoming the mainstay of the market. They created a Chinese formula for building the designer brands in China. They helped the dreams of many Chinese designers come true. Congratulations to all the practitioners! And we hope we will see some of their businesses successfully selling in the international market in the next decade.

The third generation is emerging, but still has a long journey ahead. I hope they stand firm to their dreams!

Nor should we forget those other players who have made great contributions to the development of the industry: the associations, the entrepreneurs and the college educators. Great appreciation goes to the international designers who brought fashion to China, sharing their invaluable experience with the Chinese people, and supported and engaged in the evolution of the industry.

None of this would have happened without the backing of our great country! Reformers and revolutionaries deserve to be remembered for their contributions.

China's prominence as a nation is in general accelerating world-wide. Its local culture and local talents attract the attention of other countries, and advancements in technology and science are shrinking the world.

Does this mean Chinese designers are becoming a competitive force in the fashion universe now? Will Chinese fashion designers' labels be appreciated by the Western market commercially soon? Will a designer from China become an icon in the international market in the near future?

It does seem like Chinese fashion designers are enjoying more advantages today. Their strongest advantage is—no surprise here—that China is the largest and fastest-growing country in the world. China is becoming an international market—a market everyone wants to occupy. Native Chinese designers have the advantage in surviving and sustaining their businesses in a local market.

But, this is not all there is to the story. While China is quickly building up its designer teams and brands, designer brands in other countries are emerging as well: Elley Kishimoto, Zac Posen, Alexandra Wang, to name a few. Within the sophisticated Western brand-building infrastructure, they can be branded in a much shorter period of time.

We also have to be careful about the fast pace of the industry in China. Fast does not always mean good. However, fast is what people want. They are impatient for quick growth, and the anxiety of achieving fame and profit could eventually kill talent.

In the Western world, the clothing industry experienced at least 200 years of cutting and tailoring, then about 100 years of couturier development, and now nearly 50 years of fashion design. Compared to the Western world, China has only 30 years of history in design. Westerners still enjoy their history, education and business management advantage, not counting the funding as an advantage, too. What should not be ignored is the integration ability of the Western brands in terms of designers collaborating with buyers, journalists and other marketing players.

To transform a design talent to a successful designer brand is truly a complex undertaking, involving many different factors. However, China isn't the only country with challenges. Designers like Jean Paul Gautier, Rei Kawakubo, Issey Miyake, Tom Ford and Marc Jacobs are successful, in both creativity and profit. But what about John Galliano? There's no question that his clothes gain the most interest and buzz from the media every season, but can he turn a profit? In this context, he probably should be counted as a good marketing tool for attracting public attention, rather than directly generating profits for the brand. What, then, should be the benchmark for evaluating designers? Creativity or sales numbers?

At the end of the day we're left with a question: does business decide the destiny of design, or does design decide the destiny of business? What talks the loudest—money or design? When Tom Ford surprisingly split with Gucci, he astonished the industry and caused many rumors. One popular explanation was that he failed to achieve agreement on his contract negotiations with the company. It saddened so many of his fans. He was such a cult figure that no one believed Gucci could have let him go. Ford had saved the brand from imminent death and made it a flourishing concern again. If Gucci could let a man like that go, it seems business ultimately decides the destiny of designers instead of the other way around.

One of the challenges ahead for designers is to sustain the cultural heritage and precious tailoring and sewing handicraft—especially for the Haute Couture. With globalization increasing, products, and sometimes even culture, are getting standardized and unified. If you take off the label, can you tell the designers' articles apart? How many of the young people in the world still know the history of their homelands and traditional cultures of their nations? How many of them still have the patience to learn the couture sewing and tailoring techniques? Will we create machines that can duplicate the old craftsmanship before it fades to extinction?

Our fast-moving, swift-changing times are also affecting the overall quality of the industry, in both products and services. If everyone is rushing to make more money, how can they create quality products?

Last but not least, price wars are now happening due to the current global economic crisis. Let us hope the pricing competition does not last. Who knows how long the economic crisis will last and how it will affect the designer brands' market?

If we are a globalized planet, then everyone is in the same predicament, no matter where each of us is from! So here's my advice to designers everywhere: 'Do what you like to do, and keep moving! Don't give up! You will win the game!'

NOTES

Chapter 1   Introduction

1. *Manchu* is a minority tribe in China, which built the Qing regime in 1616 and continued to rule the entire country until the end of 1911.
2. The Planned Economic System is an economic system in which the central government or workers' councils manage the economy.
3. The Rustication Movement started in the 1950s and continued through to the end of the Cultural Revolution in 1976. It sent the educated youth, normally with high-school degrees, into rural areas to assume a peasant life. On the one hand, it supported the development of remote areas, but on the other hand, it deprived young people of the opportunity to receive further education.

Chapter 2   The 1980s: The First Generation—Pioneers

1. The Great Leap Forward was a movement (1958–1961) aimed at rapidly transforming China from a primarily agrarian economy to a modern communist society.
2. The Three Years of Natural Catastrophe (1959–1962) were caused by both the natural disasters of flood and drought and misguided policies. Millions of people died of hunger and from the natural disasters.
3. The Mogao Grottoes is a famous, as well as the largest, Buddhist relic. Built in AD 366, it is located in northwest China.
4. The One Hundred Children were teenage boys dispatched to America to study by the Qing government from 1872–1875. These boys spent fifteen years in America and many of them entered Harvard, Yale and Columbia universities. The children eventually became the pundits and core revolutionists for the modernization of China.

Chapter 3   The 1990s: The Second Generation—Practitioners

1. A Socialist Market Economy is an economic form in which the major industries are owned by state entities with a minority part owned by private and/or foreigner-invested companies, and all units compete with each other within a pricing system set by the market. It differs from the old Planned Economic System largely in the aspect of price competition strategy, which used to be controlled by the central government.
2. FEC, standing for foreign exchange certificate, is a type of currency. Foreign exchange certificates are used by governments as a surrogate for a national currency, where the national currency is usually subject to exchange controls or is not convertible.
3. The Residence Card system (*Hukou* in Chinese) is a household registration record that officially identifies a person as a resident of an area. The residence card relates to a person's social welfare, children's

education and the areas where he or she can work. The residence card system is particularly restricted in big cities like Shanghai and Beijing. To get the residence card of the macro cities is the dream of many labourers from small cities or remote countryside areas.

4. '"Wu" in Chinese means "no", "not have" or "without". "Wei" means "do" or "act" in Chinese. *Wu Wei,* an ideology from Taoism, means natural action—as planets revolve around the sun, they "do" this revolving, but without "doing" it; or as trees grow, they "do", but without "doing". Thus knowing when (and how) to act is not knowledge in the sense that one would think "now" is the right time to do "this", but rather just doing it, doing the natural thing'. (Wikipedia, en.wikipedia.org/wiki/ Wu-wei, accessed 30 September 2009.)

Chapter 4   The Twenty-first Century: The Third Generation—Prospects

1. The One-child Policy issued in 1979 mandated one child per family in order to properly control the quickly growing population.
2. *Project Runway,* hosted by supermodel Heidi Klum, is an American reality television series focusing on fashion design.

BIBLIOGRAPHY

Archive Q243–4-1, the Shanghai Archive Center.

Bai, Sha. (1998), 'Spread the Wings: Interview with the Fashion Designer Wu Hai-Yan (*Zhankai tengfei de chibang: ji fuzhuang shejishi Wu Hai-Yan*)', *People's Daily (Renmin ribao)*, 19 October, p. 12.

Chen, Jie. (2007), 'Kicking Open the Door to Paris,' 21 July, accessed 30 September 2009, http://www.fashionencyclopedia.com/Le-Ma/Matsuda-Mitsuhiro.html

Gu, Jun. (2000), 'Wang Xin-Yuan: The Beautiful Life (*Wang Xin-Yuan: meili rensheng*)', *International Aviation News (Guoji hangkong bao)*, 22 May, p. 10.

Harper's Bazaar China. (2008), 'The First Chinese Icon at the Paris Fashion Week (*Bali shizhuangzhou shang diyi zhang zhongguo pai*)', *Harper's Bazaar China (Shishang Basha)*, 173/6: 13.

Jewel. (2008), 'Liang Zi, the Chinese Fashion Master of Environmental Protection (*Liang Zi, zhongguo shizhuang huanbao dashi*)', *Harper's Bazaar China (Shishang Basha)*, 169/2: 150.

Li, Bao-Jian, and Jin Jing. (2008), 'The Beauty of Fall/Winter 08/09 Paris Fashion Week, China Fashion Show (*Qiudong Zhi Mei-Ji 08/09 Bali Qiudong Shizhuangzhou, Xiuchang Zhongguo*)', *Elle (China)*, 5: 104.

Li, Man-Xun, and Mao Li-Hui. (2006), 'Liu Yang—The Player in Fashion Regime, Bearing His Mission (*Liu Yang—beifu shiming de shishang wuzhe*)', *Chinese Textile News (Zhongguo fangzhi bao)*, 1 December, p. 5.

Li, Shuo. (2000), 'Models Strut Their Stuff on the Great Wall', *China Daily (Zhongguo ribao)*, 24 June, p. 10.

Li, Xiang. (1994), 'Liu Yang—The Chinese Pioneering Fashion Designer (*Liu Yang—zhongguo xianfeng pai shizhuang sheji Shi*)', *The Oriental Arts (Dongfang yishu)*, 6: 28.

Liu, Li-Fang. (2008), 'Liang Zi—Refreshing the Most Expensive Silk with the Legacy Techniques from Ming Dynasty (*Liang Zi, yong mingdai gongyi zaixian zui anggui de sichou*)', *Bund Picture (Waitan huabao)*, 28 August, p. B36.

Man, man. (2005), 'The Local Young Design Talent—Lu Kun (*Bencheng xinrui shejishi—Lu Kun*)', *Shanghai Times (Shengjiang fuwu daobao)*, 6 April, p. F03.

Mao, Jing-Bo. (1992), 'Wang's Designs Hot with Working Women', *China Daily (Zhongguo ribao)*, 22 April, p. 4.

Qi, Lin. (1998), 'The Fashion Tour Show, Blowing in the Wind (*Shizhuang xunhuizhan, guaqi haoda feng*)', *China Youth Daily (Zhongguo qinnian bao)*, 5 June, p. 6.

Shui, Mi-Tao. (2008), 'China Fashion Meets with Western Fashion—A Look at the 2008 Shanghai Fashion Week (*Zhongwai shishang de duijie rouhe—2008 Shanghai shizhuangzhou yi pie*)', *Evening Newspaper (Xinwen wanbao)*, 14 November, p. B20.

Sina.com. (2005), 'Top 100 Figures in Shanghai Fashion Regime—Wang Yi-Yang (*Shanghai shishang quanli 100 ren, Wang Yi-Yang*)', 27 September, accessed 5 March 2009, http://eladies.sina.com.cn/nx/2005/0927/1933195787.html

Wang, Dong-Xia. (2003), *From Chinese Robe and Jacket to Western-style Suits (Cong changpao magua dao xizhuang gelü)*, Sichuan: Sichuan People's Publishing Firm.

Wu, Dong-Yan. (2006), 'Ma Ke—The Lonely Anchoress in the Noisy City (*Ma Ke—xuanxiao chengshi de jijing yinzhe*)', *Elle (China)*, 3: 152.

Xiao, Hui. (2007), 'A New Exception in Paris (*Chuangru Bali de Sheji Meixue*)', *Vogue (China)*, 72/3: 156.

Xie, Yi. (2007), 'The Spider Man—Ji Ji (*Zhizhu ren Ji Ji*)', 8 March, accessed 5 March 2009, http://www.cnci.gov.cn/news/design/news_4628.htm

Xinhua Net. (2008), 'Wu Hai-Yan: The Fashion Designer Inspired by the National Spirit (*Wu Hai-Yan, yong minzu jinsheng chuangyi de fuzhuang shejishi*)', 19 December, accessed 5 March 2009, http://news.xinhuanet.com/photo/2008–12/19/content_10528985.htm

Xu, Zhu-Qing. (1983), 'Clean the Spiritual Contamination vs. Beautify Life' (*Wuran bixu Qingchu, Shenghuo yao meihua*)', *China Youth Daily (Zhongguo Qingnian Bao)*, 17 November, p. 1.

Yan, Fei. (2008), 'Xie Fen, the Chinese Mainstay (*Xie Fen, Zhongguo Shi Zhuliu*)', *Harper's Bazaar China (Shishang Basha)*, 172/5: 189.

Zhu, Ye. (1956), 'In the Garment Factory (*Zai fuzhuang gongchang li*)', *New People Evening Paper (Xinmin Wanbao)*, 29 February, p. 2.

REFERENCE LIST

Archives in the Shanghai Archive Centre
Beijing Youth Daily
China Daily
China Youth Daily
Elle (*China*)
Harper's Bazaar (*China*)
Shanghai Fashion Times (*Shanghai shizhuang bao*)
Vogue (*China*)
www.chiconline.com.cn (official Web site of China International Clothes and Accessory
    Fair, CHIC)
www.fashion.org.cn (official Web site of China International Fashion Week)
www.liuyang.com.cn (Web site of designer Liu Yang)
www.mixmind.com.cn (Web site of designer Ma Ke)
www.poledesign.cn (Web site of designer Ji Ji)
www.shtong.gov.cn (official Web site of *Shanghai Chronicles*)
www.tangy.com.cn (Web site of designer Liang Zi)
info.texnet.com.cn (China textile Web site)
www.why-design.com (Web site of designer Wu Hai-Yan)
www.zuczug.com (Web site of designer Wang Yi-Yang)

INDEX

Shaan Xi, 139, 142
Shanghai, 1, 3, 9–16, 20–7 passim, 34–46
    passim, 51, 60, 70, 93, 99, 139, 188,
    213–24 passim, 234, 242n3
    Apparel Group, 18
    Archive Centre 5–6, 10–11, 13, 18
    Fashion Festival, 24
    Garment Company, 33
    Garment Research Centre, 18
    International Fashion Federation, 36, 64,
        214
    International Fashion Festival, 25, 140
Shangri-La Gala, 217
Shanshan Garment Group, 36
Shanshan Group, 37, 46
Shaoxing, 139
Shenzhen, 20, 36, 42–3, 94, 139, 141, 143,
    148, 168, 214
    Fashion Designers Contest, 42
Shi Kai, 33
Shu Liang Silk, 140, 144–7, 163
Sidima, 121
silk, 4, 6, 57, 64–72 passim, 81–2, 86, 93–4,
    108, 116, 148 *see also* Shu Liang Silk
Singapore, 22, 210, 217, 224
    Fashion Festival, 217, 224
Sino–France Cultural Week, 69, 110, 215
Sino–France Fashion Week, 69, 85
Sino–U.S Cultural Week, 69
Sinyuan, 37, 44–50
socialismus, 15–20, 31, 137, 141n1
Socialist Market Economy, 137, 241n1
Song Huai-Jia, 32
Southeast Asia, 109–10
Soviet Union, 16–18
sports wear, 17
State Council, 32, 43, 70
state-owned enterprise, 15, 26, 31, 34, 39,
    42–3, 116, 137, 143–5 passim, 210
Strategic Development Plan of Clothing
    Industry, 137
Sui, Anna, 214
suit
    Lenin-, 15–16
    Mao-, 15–16
    Western-style, 4, 6, 9–10, 17
    Zhong-Shan, 6, 9, 16
Sun Yat-Sen, 6

Suzhou, 57, 164
    Institute of Silk Science, 20, 36, 39–40, 164
Sweden, 145

tailor, 3–5, 9–18 passim, 21–2, 46, 96, 105,
    116–18 passim, 142, 216–17, 238
Tailor's Shop, 10
tailoring technique, 11, 33, 239
Taiwan, 130, 210
Tam, Vivian, 217
Tangy, 29, 138–41, 143–5, 148, 163
Tax Bureau, 12
theatre, 14, 94, 213
'The Generation of Prosperity', 71
Three Years of Natural Catastrophe, 37
Tian Jia-Dong, 15–16
Tianjin, 3
Tianyi Ge, 55, 57
Tianzifang, 214
Tokyo, 91–6, 216
    Fashion Week, 69, 215
Top Five Chinese Fashion Designer Award,
    108
Top Ten Fashion Designers Awards, 36, 69,
    108, 144
Top Ten National Excellence of Young
    Designers Award, 140
trade
    barrier, 27, 167
    fair, 23, 25, 33–4, 36, 40, 69, 109, 138
Tsing-Hua University of Fine Arts, 34
Tu Wen-An, 126–8

'Underoath', 228–33
UNESCO, 36
Ungaro, 129
uniform, 6, 15–17, 19, 38, 108, 111, 220
United States, 10, 22, 43, 64, 69, 93, 96, 138,
    167, 220, 241n4
'Useless', 165, 169–87, 215

Vanh Wan, 219–20
Victoria and Albert Museum, 165, 169, 189,
    215, 217, 224
Vietnam, 43
'Vision 2002', 65, 83–4
Vogue, 14, 215
Vuitton, Louis, 1, 137, 215

ABOUT THE AUTHOR

Photographer: Vanh Wan

Christine Tsui obtained her master's degree in Fashion Marketing and Management from the London College of Fashion in 2003. Now she is a managing director of a local Chinese fashion brand. Christine is also a visiting lecturer in the Shanghai Institute of China Academy of Arts. She has published books (in Chinese) including: *Wedding Gown: Let the Gown Witness Your Love; Tailors' Story: from Tailors to Top Designers; Dialogue with Chinese Designers of Three Generations: Pursuing the Dream* (Shanghai designers only).